Changes and Challenges

Economic Transformation
in East-Central Europe

Changes and Challenges

Economic Transformation in East-Central Europe

Edited by
Pál Gáspár

Akadémiai Kiadó, Budapest

English text edited by
Péter Tamási

ISBN 963 05 6987 6

© Pál Gáspár, 1995

Published by Akadémiai Kiadó, H–1117 Budapest, Prielle Kornélia u. 19–35.

Printed in Hungary by
MSZH Nyomda és Kiadó Kft.

Contents

Introduction

This volume is the first attempt of a research team of the Institute for World Economics of the Hungarian Academy of Sciences at monitoring key issues of economic development and development policies in the more advanced countries in transition.

The applied approach is based on two essential findings. First, it has been increasingly felt that the traditional tools of short-term economic analysis, regularly applied for developed and less developed countries alike, cannot be used with the same accuracy and predictability in the case of the countries in transition. Transformation is a long and qualitative process which cannot be adequately described by short-term and quantitative methods. And it is even more important: short-term indicators may often turn out to be completely misleading, with serious consequences for the economic policy-making process. Secondly, both the classical tools of economic surveys and the approaches chosen for the description of the transformation process have largely concentrated on macroeconomic trends and figures. Also the traditional national and international statistical systems mainly offer macroeconomic data. We, however, are convinced that the sustainable success of the transformation fundamentally depends on microeconomic adjustment. Therefore, the regular survey and the explanation of the microeconomic trends are indispensable for identifying the progress or the failure of the transformation process and for providing useful analyses and suggestions to policy-makers.

The studies contained in this volume tried to follow this "philosophy". On the one hand, they *analyse medium-term economic processes,* as much as experience and lessons from the first five years of transformation allow such an approach. On the other hand, *microeconomic considerations* have been taken into account when selecting the topics to be dealt with. Thus, there is a justified hope that the risks of applying – never valid – textbook economy recipes and of identifying daily developments with longer-term trends can be substantially reduced. In consequence, the obvious gap between most traditional economic analyses and the economic reality of the transformation can be narrowed, economic policy-makers can be equipped with background materials of a somewhat better quality, and, finally, also scholars can be given the opportunity to better understand the real nature of the transformation.

An additional novelty of the approach is its *comparative nature.* All issues have been examined on a regional level, covering the Czech Republic, Hungary, Poland, Slovakia and Slovenia.

This volume contains eight papers dealing with monetary and exchange rate policies, foreign trade, labour market developments, the financial system, the role of foreign direct investments, company-level adjustment and agriculture in the transformation process.

Ervin Apáthy's study concentrates on the *inflationary developments* in the economies in transition and on the *applied monetary policies*. Developments in inflation and the changes in its pattern are important, since they strongly influence the costs of economic transition. In the initial period of the transition, all economies experienced a big increase in the inflation, as the consumer and producer subsidies became reduced and the prices liberalized. In addition, the exchange rate was steeply devalued to reduce the import demand after the opening of the economies. This initial growth of inflation was different in the countries having applied shock therapy and in those having introduced gradualism. In the former case the corrective inflation meant a rapid and short-term price increase, while in the latter case this initial jump was less pronounced.

Later, the inflation was reduced but it is still high as compared to developed market economies. Double-digit inflation rates are dangerous, since they can rapidly develop to even higher ones. The problem is that the underlying core inflation is high and it has been reproduced from year to year. It might be stimulated by wage increases, the adjustment of the exchange rate or by the upward adjustment of administrative prices.

Important changes have occurred both in the legal status of the central banks and in the applied tools of monetary policy. The central banks were fully dependent on the fiscal policy in the centrally planned economies and the reforms were directed at establishing their independence from the central government by regulating the amount of deficit that may be financed by the central bank. The tools of monetary policy have also changed much: the initial instruments of liquidity regulation like interest rates or compulsory reserves have been replaced by more market-oriented instruments of open market operations, foreign and domestic currency swaps, etc. Nevertheless, both the goals and the instruments are changing, which creates uncertainty and reduces the credibility of the monetary policy.

Pál Gáspár analyses the different *exchange rate policies* pursued by the economies in transition. Exchange rate policies play a crucial role in macroeconomic stabilization, in the opening of the economies as well as in microeconomic restructuring.

Having presented the theoretical background of the choice of exchange rate policies in the economies in transition, the chapter reviews the practical experiences with exchange rate policies. According to the criteria set by the literature for optimum currency areas, these economies should follow relatively similar exchange rate policies. However, one can identify a great diversity in this respect, as the Czech Republic has a fixed exchange rate, Poland a preannounced crawling peg, Slovakia and Hungary have an adjustable peg, while a free float is the rule in Slovenia. The reasons for the differences in the choice of the exchange rate policies are related to the initial macroeconomic imbalances, the scope of former liberalization, as well as the speed and sequencing of the stabilization measures.

The chapter then surveys individual exchange rate policies, including the choice of currency basket, the relationship between the exchange rate and other macroeconomic policies, and the various stages of the exchange rate developments.

The author points out that there are also common trends in the national exchange rate developments. Among them, the appreciation of the real exchange rate, the increasing conflict between the goals of curbing inflation and supporting exports, and the necessity of changes in the applied exchange rate policies are mentioned.

Foreign trade developments are of crucial importance for the countries in transition. Magdolna Sass points out that this sector is expected to become one of the most important engines of technological modernization, economic restructuring and growth. At a first glance, all countries were successful in reorienting their trade towards the developed market economies, mainly to the European Union (EU), and within it, towards Germany. In this process, all of them have come closer to the "normal" geographical and commodity pattern of trade, determined on the basis of theories of international economics (gravity model) and historical experience. However, after 1993, the dynamism of this process has slowed down substantially. Neither can changes in the commodity pattern be considered completed. While there are encouraging shifts towards reaching a commodity composition based on production factor endowments, material- and energy-intensive products still dominate the pattern of exports.

While at the beginning, changes in conditions of market access contributed to the successful reorientation of trade, after 1993 there has been no significant change in this respect. Moreover, with growing protectionist tendencies in almost all of the important purchasing markets, the economies in transition have seen their market access changing adversely. Due to the substantially different volume of traded goods, this barrier cannot be counterbalanced by better access to each other's markets. Also the markets offered by the successor states of the Soviet Union may provide better prospects in a longer run only.

It is stressed that in the field of foreign trade performance, the internal factors play an equally or even more important role than the external ones.

Klára Fóti reviews the situation on the *labour market* in the Visegrád countries and Slovenia. The paper highlights specific employment and unemployment problems in those Central European economies which started their transition earlier. As a result of the rapid rise in unemployment, labour market institutions have been established and a wide range of measures introduced. However, there still remain several problems which cannot be adequately addressed by these policy measures, for they are deeply rooted in the previous economic and social system.

One set of problems is associated with the extremely high degree of rigidity of the labour market inherited from past decades. Although many of the previous causes of institutional rigidity started to be abolished, labour mobility, skills and forms of employment cannot be changed overnight. Moreover, neither the current macroeconomic constraints facilitate changes. On the contrary, they sometimes add to the slow adjustment of labour. Amidst deep recession, the private sector's employment-generating capacity remains limited, real interest rates are high and demand is still contracting for large sections of the population.

The other set of problems is connected with the expanding hidden economy. This is all the more important, since it is closely associated with polarization among the unemployed. People having competitive skills are much less vulnerable than the unskilled or those with obsolete skills. The author calls for active labour market measures of a more targeting nature.

In addition, broader macroeconomic issues should also be taken into account, as they influence labour market developments to a great extent. This fact has not been recognized so far, and thus it has contributed to aggravating the unemployment problems. Attention is drawn to the role of taxation in the shaping of adequate fiscal policies, in line with the objective of encouraging employment by lowering labour costs.

György Csáki deals with the developments in the *financial sector,* including both the banking system and the capital markets. The study reviews the most important common and country-specific trends, the achieved results and the current obstacles hampering the more successful development of this sector.

9

The most important structural changes in the banking system are analysed from the time of the establishment of the two-tier banking systems. The treatment of the bad loan issue and the privatization of the commercial banks are also dealt with in this chapter. Notwithstanding the chosen options ("indirect recapitalization" in Poland, transfer of bad loans into a specific state bank in the former Czechoslovakia, and recapitalization with government bonds in Hungary), the bad loans still represent a high share of the credit supply and the GDP, and they are further increasing. The privatization of the commercial banks has already begun, but only a few of them have virtually been privatized in Poland and Hungary. The "privatized" banks in the Czech Republic and Slovakia have actually not been restructured.

The author explains why the banking system could not substantially contribute to the promotion of growth in the private sector. Among the most important factors, he identifies the crowding out impact of fiscal imbalances, the high risks associated with the financing of the emerging new ventures and the absence of risk-sharing mechanisms.

Finally, the chapter pays attention to developments in the capital markets. In this context, trends in the Czech Republic are encouraging due to the voucher-type privatization. Nevertheless, the high concentration of ownership, the impact of foreign capital inflow on the volatility of share prices and turnovers, as well as inconsistencies between the supply and demand remain important constraints. In Hungary and Poland the development of capital markets is restricted by the virtual absence of institutional investors, the high fiscal deficits and the lack of sufficient supply of assets to be offered by state-owned and private or privatized firms.

István Mádi's study analyses the inflow of *foreign direct capital* into the economies in transition. This process is very important, since these economies have been historically poor in capital and both their modernization and the overcoming of the present recession depend on the supply of investable funds provided by foreign capital.

The author evaluates the current experiences of the economies in transition with the volume, composition and dynamics of capital inflow. He also gives a comparative analysis explaining similarities and differences in the national strategies which are focussed on attracting foreign direct investors. The paper elaborates on the structural features of the capital inflow, identifying those sectors that could absorb the relatively highest amount of foreign capital. In this context the author finds significant similarities between the individual economies.

With respect to the amount of invested capital, the paper points out that about half of all investments have come to Hungary. This development is explained by the relatively better state of microeconomic reforms and the progress already made in corporate restructuring.

Finally, the national policies to stimulate foreign investors are dealt with. The author determines the key areas of macroeconomic policies, of privatization strategies and microeconomic reforms that are and remain preconditions of achieving the expected and necessary volume of foreign capital inflow in the coming years.

The state and the tasks of *microeconomic adjustment* in the economies under transformation have been examined by Miklós Szanyi. The author stresses that this transformation has to be seen within the framework of the complex historical modernization efforts. From the viewpoint of companies, there are unprecedented challenges; these include the existence of obsolete technologies and products, a heritage of 45-year-long isolation from the developed world; sudden exposure to external competition due to quick and unilateral liberalization measures; recession in the domestic and Eastern markets; the decline of public procurement and military-related sales; lack of financial means for development in historically undercapitalized economies facing a severe credit crunch; and, finally, inadequate corporate and management structures.

The immediate consequences of these changes have been manifested in a substantial drop in production, rapidly rising unemployment and the liquidity crisis of companies.

Barriers to microeconomic adjustment can be reduced by reshaping the legal and institutional framework, including the dissolution of system-specific elements causing soft budget constraints, paternalistic relationships and inadequate ownership structures. In addition, the companies' liquidity problems have to be eased to enable them to finance modernization. Also the government has to provide support to strengthen companies through special development agencies.

The author underlines that the success of microeconomic adjustment in the individual economies crucially depends on the initial conditions. In fact, they have been largely different in the Central and the Southeast European countries. In the first years of transformation, only in Central Europe could positive trends in adjustment and favourable changes in ownership and corporate governance structures be observed. These shifts occurred irrespective of the fact that different privatization methods were applied. In addition, the genuine private sector experienced a significantly quicker development in Central Europe.

Judit Kiss provides a comparative survey of the *crisis and transformation of agriculture in East-Central Europe*. She points out that the crisis in the agriculture of the economies in transition is not only a production crisis characterized by lower output levels or declining capital and labour efficiency. It can only be explained if structural, institutional and ownership features are also considered.

In the last years, signs of a crisis have manifested themselves in various areas. The rapid opening of the so-called agricultural scissors and the subsequent worsening of the domestic terms of trade, deterioration in the efficiency of the use of the factors of production, a decrease in the self-financing capacity of the agricultural sector, growing indebtedness of the agricultural units, and increasing dismissals and unemployment can be mentioned in this context. In a medium-term retrospection, the reasons for this crisis can be found in the overall development policy which hampered the growth of agriculture, the significant capital outflow from this sector, the continuous decrease of subsidies and other means of financial support, and in the one-sided market orientation of production.

In the economies in transition, the establishment of appropriate market structures and the introduction of efficient market regulation are of crucial importance. The liberalization of agricultural trade has to be reconsidered. Recent experience clearly shows that liberalization proved to be an ambiguous instrument in agriculture in East-Central Europe. Although initially it increased exports to some extent, but imports grew much more rapidly and threaten to substantially reduce or even eliminate strategically important production activities.

Finally, the paper presents the most important ways of the ownership reform in agriculture, including restitution, the privatization of state-owned co-operatives and farms, and it also deals with the liquidation and bankruptcy procedures initiated against agricultural units.

Budapest, September 1995

András Inotai
Director of the Institute
for World Economics of the
Hungarian Academy of Sciences

Inflation and monetary policy in the "Visegrád countries" and Slovenia

Ervin Apáthy

Initial macroeconomic conditions

At the beginning of the period considered (1989–1994), beside a number of similar features, there were also considerable differences in the economies of the Visegrád countries and Slovenia. First of all, we shall identify some of those conditions which diverged in the "Visegrád countries" (the Czech Republic, Hungary, Poland, Slovakia) and Slovenia and which later influenced price level developments.

Former Czechoslovakia already implemented cautious macroeconomic management in the communist era. Fiscal and credit policies were conservative and budgetary subsidies to state-owned companies were relatively small. Also foreign debt was kept relatively low. As a result, domestic imbalances were smaller than in most countries of the region. Both recorded and hidden inflation were low. Excess demand had not built up in the form of a large monetary overhang. From the macroeconomic point of view, Czechoslovakia enjoyed perhaps the best initial conditions for reform in East-Central Europe.

Slovakia, within the former Czechoslovak Federation was, on the one hand, subject to the extreme centralization efforts of Czechoslovak communist leaders and, on the other hand, could enjoy the traditionally moderate and conservative fiscal and monetary management. As a result, Slovakia entered the period considered with relatively favourable macroeconomic conditions. However, it had to face the shock of the consequences of its new independence as well, the most important ones of which in my view were the termination of fiscal transfers from the Czech Republic and that it had to build up its central institutions of economic management (among them a central bank) from, in fact, a non-existing base.

At the beginning of the period, Hungary was at a more advanced stage in the creation of a market economy than the other countries of the region (a two-tier banking system existed, the basis of a modern tax system had been introduced and a comprehensive liberalization process was carried on, etc.). On the macroeconomic side, however, despite its continuous gradualist approach and avoidance of abrupt changes, serious imbalances existed in the economy: a high external debt accumulated and the country has lived with a double digit inflation rate since 1988.

In Poland and former Yugoslavia, hyper-inflation emerged in late 1989 and stabilization of the economy had become the most important concern by 1990.

The credibility of the Polish economic policy had seriously eroded by 1989; the large budget deficit and the extensive price indexation of wages resulted in near hyper-inflation (30% a month). Following the correction measures in late 1989, at the beginning of 1990 monetary and wage policy was further tightened, budgetary cuts and price corrections were carried out and the exchange rate became fixed.

13

The macroeconomic situation in former Yugoslavia at the end of 1989 was very similar to that in Poland. The initial conditions for the creation of a new currency were determined by the failure of the shock therapy stabilization programme of late 1989, which was introduced by the former Yugoslav government with a fixed exchange rate, a tight monetary policy and wage controls having been the pillars. After the initial success, the programme failed, the main reasons having been the initial overvaluation of the dinar, inconsistency (the programme was left without consistent built-in nominal anchors), the weakness of wage controls and monetary overhang. Policy-makers started to pump money into the system and to increase wage levels. The severe monetary restrictions were not able to counterbalance the increase in private and public spending, and price stability became unsustainable. All these failures ended in a recession without deflation.

The restrictive practice of the former Yugoslav monetary policy collapsed in 1990. The mistakes of the National Bank of Yugoslavia resulted in a high dinar liquidity in the former Yugoslav banks. The collapse of the economic reform was perhaps one of the main reasons for the break up of the Federation.

Slovenia, introducing its own currency, has become an economically independent country from October 8, 1991. Although Slovenia had established a limited sovereignty in its fiscal and foreign exchange system long before the formal proclamation of independence, the possibilities for keeping track of its monetary aggregates were limited. A separate monetary system was the final step towards its full economic independence.

Price level developments

Price level developments have been one of the main problems and policy concerns in the Visegrád countries and Slovenia. While at the beginning of the period considered the magnitude of inflation rates in Poland and the former Yugoslavia differed significantly from that of the other Visegrád countries and Slovenia, since then inflation rates have converged, having stabilized at a still high annual level everywhere (20–35%), although the Polish inflation rates are still higher.

In Poland, the stabilization programme allowed for some initial inflation to dry out monetary overhang. The January 1990 inflation rate was almost 80%. Soon after that, substantial reduction in price increase was achieved and by the second half of the year, the monthly inflation rate was 3–6%, but still much higher than targeted. The annual inflation rate was 584.7%.

In former Yugoslavia, after an initial success inflation had accelerated by the end of 1990. In former Czechoslovakia, the first price shock occurred in 1990. Although economic policy had carefully prepared the subsidy eliminations and the administrative price increases in 1990, the annual inflation rate was 10.1%, anyway by far the lowest among the Visegrád countries and Slovenia in that year.

Hungarian economic policy, well ahead in the liberalization process, had to face a 29% price increase in 1990.

In 1991, the inflation rate in Poland continued to slow down, while in former Yugoslavia the government completely lost control of inflation.

Czechoslovakia experienced an extreme price shock of almost 58% in 1991. Hungary also reached a peak in price increases, of 35% that year. Compared to 1991, yearly inflation markedly fell down in 1992 in all countries except Slovenia where inflation accelerated at the annual level. In 1993, the price increase decelerated everywhere in the region, especially in Poland and Slovenia, but the Czech Republic and Slovakia passed the 20% mark.

The producer price pattern has been somewhat different. Producer prices grew much faster than consumer prices after the price liberalization, but following the initial price shock, they rose more slowly.

As seen above, although overall inflation remained relatively high everywhere and rates fluctuated significantly over the period, inflation behaviour in all the Visegrád countries and Slovenia has broadly followed similar paths.

Price level developments in all of the countries considered can be divided into at least two well identifiable periods. Repressed inflation in many countries under central planning turned into open inflation after the introduction of the reform programmes, which was followed by a deceleration of the price increase. Except for Hungary, there was an initial price shock in the countries of the region, which coincided with the introduction of the reform packages. The price increase then soon came down to a much lower level. The initial price shock turned out to be substantially larger than expected. In Hungary, inflation had gradually accelerated since the late 1980s and after a 35% peak in 1991, it started to decelerate at an annual level. In Slovenia, the overall trend differs due to the dissolution process of former Yugoslavia. The fluctuation of the inflation rate has been higher there than elsewhere and after the early 1990 price jump there was an "additional" hyper-inflationary period from about mid-1991 to mid 1992.

In Czechoslovakia, the price increase was moderate until January 1991. Then after an initial price shock at the beginning of 1991, from the second quarter of the year the price increase was significantly lower throughout 1991 and 1992. Following a smaller price shock at the beginning of 1993, inflation was controlled until the end of the year. In 1990, consumer prices rose by 10.1% over the year. Price developments following the January 1, 1991 big bang have had two well identifiable stages: an initial price jump after the price liberalization, followed by a stabilization of the price growth rate and the annual level of consumer price index which had increased to 158%. The initial price jump was finished in March, and later the inflation was brought under control. Prices continued to increase after February, but at a decelerating rate. In 1992, economic policy succeeded in keeping the inflation rate under 12%.

In Slovakia, price developments were very similar to those observed in the whole of Czechoslovakia until the end of 1992: after an initial price jump in early 1991, inflation was kept under control in the rest of 1991 and also in 1992.

In Hungary, consumer prices increased by 28.9% in 1990. The Hungarian economy experienced the highest inflation in 1991. The annual average level of consumer prices was 35% higher than in 1990, however, the industrial sales price level exceeded the December 1990 price level by only 16.8%. The inflation, taking into consideration producer prices, reached its peak in the first months of 1991. The peak of consumer price increase was reached in the middle of 1991 after which inflation slowed down in both terms until the end of 1991 and the beginning of 1992. In the autumn of 1992 inflation accelerated again. Consumer price developments were similar. From the beginning of 1992 monthly inflation rates were decreasing until July, then inflation increased to a small extent and became consolidated by December. The average monthly price increase in 1992 was 1.7% as against 2.5% in 1991. The consumer price level of December 1992 was 23% higher than that of December 1991.

15

In Poland, the price increase shows a somewhat similar picture, however, magnitudes are different. Consumer prices rose by 584.7% in 1990, 70.3% in 1991, 43.0% in 1992 and 35.3% in 1993 (see Table 1).

By the end of 1991, Slovenia – within the former Yugoslav Federation – was experiencing a starting hyper-inflation. Soon after the declaration of independence, by the second half of 1992, the Slovenian authorities succeeded to bring down the average monthly inflation rate to 2.2%. After a further deceleration of inflation, the annual inflation rate fluctuated at around 24% in the last months of 1993. Similarly, neither the monthly inflation rates exceeded the 2% growth rate in a greater part of the year (except for winter months).

Table 1
Annual consumer price changes from 1990 to 1993 (%)

	1990	1991	1992	1993
Czech Republic	9.7	52.0	11.1	20.8
Hungary	28.9	35.0	23.0	21.1
Poland	584.7	70.3	43.0	35.3
Slovakia	10.4	58.3	10.0	25.1
Slovenia	549.7	117.7	201.3	32.3
Czechoslovakia	10.1	57.9	–	–
Former Yugoslavia	588.0	121.8	–	–

Source: National Statistics; *European Economic Survey,* UN, various years; *The Vienna Institute Monthly Report,* 1993, No. 31.

Sources and factors of inflation

Factors of inflation differ from country to country and from period to period. However, a number of common elements influencing price developments can be found. Furthermore, the relative significance of factors has changed over the last few years. Possible sources of the unexpectedly high initial price level shock and the consequent persisting inflation must be sought in a combination of factors of the supply and the demand sides.

On the supply side, many factors related to economic transformation have resulted in inflationary pressures. Transformation from a command into a market economy requires the execution of similar tasks in many respects: the transformation of the production and redistribution systems, of foreign market relations, the deregulation of investments, trade and prices, the modernization of the banking system and of taxation, and the reduction of state budget subsidies. All this implied price increases.

First of all, the consumer and producer price liberalization has to be mentioned. Price restructuring from centrally administered to basically market determined prices constituted a common element of the structural reforms. Sequencing and timing of price reforms were essential factors of price level increases as well as of the reduction and termination of subsidies.

The effects of drastic administrative increases of the controlled prices, namely, of energy and raw materials, produced sharp price increases. Effects of the subsequent removal of subsidies, the increase in indirect taxation (or more generally, tax system restructuring), and those of foreign trade liberalization on the price level have been similar: production costs grew sharply.

In some countries (Poland, Czechoslovakia, former Yugoslavia), the initial drastic devaluation of the currency and/or continuous small devaluations in other countries (Hungary, Poland), which had radically changed the relative prices, resulted in growing producer prices. Further supply side factors such as rising interest rates and continuously and drastically decreasing economic performance (mainly because expectations of large price jumps were causing substantial reduction in expected demand) had led to unit cost increase under the deepening recession.

Here again the shock treatment in Poland and the former Yugoslavia has to be distinguished from the more cautious approach of the Czechoslovak and the Hungarian policy-makers. In the former two countries, as a part of the reform package, virtually all prices were at once liberalized. The relatively successful Czechoslovak inflation performance undoubtedly had a significant role in delaying many of the liberalization measures, retaining important methods of price and foreign trade regulation and also in making it possible to hold the currency exchange rate stable after the initial devaluation.

In Hungary, liberalization had been continuous after the late 1980s, but inflation was boosted by current account imbalances and the subsequent devaluations of the national currency. Besides that, the excessive presence of monopolistic behaviour on the part of companies and its inflationary impact have also to be mentioned. Most of the above-mentioned sources have been in operation and have contributed to continuous inflation in the period considered. Our analysis suggests that "government induced" inflationary measures (administrative price adjustment, tax reforms and devaluations) are responsible for a significant part of the inflation and explain the major trends.

In some countries, also nominal variables (money, credit and wages) tended to reach a level consistent with the initially expected long-term inflation.

Wage policies affect price level both on the supply and the demand side. Generally, while at the beginning of the transition and stabilization process wage policies had a substantial anti-inflationary effect, later wage developments significantly contributed to persisting inflation. Initially, the economies of the Visegrád countries and Slovenia underwent a substantial real wage decline: 24% in Poland in 1990, 27% in Czechoslovakia and 26.5% in former Yugoslavia in 1991. Hungary is an exception, as the real wage decrease was only 1.2% in 1990 and 1.1% in 1991.

The drastic real wage decrease was soon followed by a substantial growth in Czechoslovakia (8.1%), by moderate growth in Hungary (3.9%), and by a further decrease in Poland (1.8%) and Slovenia (0.8%). Hungary's real wage pattern has been much more stable than that of the other Visegrád countries and Slovenia; its annual changes were much smaller than elsewhere.

Previously existing monetary overhang did not play a significant role, except in Poland and the former Yugoslavia. In Czechoslovakia and Hungary excess demand in the form of monetary overhang was relatively small. Actually, monetary overhang did not play a significant role anywhere after the introduction of the reform and stabilization policies.

On the other hand, decreasing inflation rates since 1991 might imply that market forces had positive supply effects. By 1992, much of the liberalization work had been completed, and budget subsidies had been significantly decreased. Another factor of the

17

deceleration of inflation was that the previously characteristic shortages in these markets ceased to exist and supply became dominant, due to import liberalization, the domestic private economy and foreign investments. All this stimulated market competition.

Monetary policies

Analysis of monetary developments is extremely difficult due to the limited availability of statistics and the differences in classification.

At the beginning of the period, monetary policies were intended to be tight in all the Visegrád countries and in Slovenia, partly because tight monetary and fiscal targets were cornerstones of all stabilization agreements with the IMF (International Monetary Fund). The scope of monetary financing was increasing due to fiscal deficits and foreign debt service, although except for Hungary and Czechoslovakia, none of the countries serviced their foreign debts fully.

In Czechoslovakia, the new political decision-makers gave absolute priority to anti-inflationary goals. In Hungary, although the necessity of disinflation was considered important, disinflationary policy was not the only priority. The freedom of Hungarian economic policy was to a large extent limited by the country's accumulated foreign debt. The number one priority objective had to be the maintenance of Hungary's solvency. Containment of the speeding up of inflation was only the second policy objective. The more favourable position of Czechoslovakia in this respect allowed for a more restrictive policy. However, monetary policies were restrictive in both countries in 1990 and 1991.

In both Poland and the former Yugoslavia, the restrictive monetary policy – particularly stopping the practice of monetizing the state budget deficits, coupled with strict wage policies and an exchange rate anchor – formed an important part of the stabilization programme. While at the beginning of 1990 monetary policy was restrictive in both countries, in the second half of the year their central banks eased monetary policies. While in Poland, monetary policy relaxed slightly, in Yugoslavia, monetary policy accommodated the mistaken fiscal and other policy measures. Money printing became the main source of revenue for the federal government and in the second half of 1991 already the total of the fiscal deficit was monetized.

After 1991, recession and inflation continued to be the main concerns for internal economic and monetary policies, causing a dilemma for decision-makers as to which one to choose as a priority.

By 1992, in all Visegrád countries and Slovenia, the general macroeconomic policy focus had shifted and attention was turned from disinflation toward a move from recession to recovery. However, anti-inflationary targets were still considered important.

Nominal growth of money supply was large in the period considered in all the examined countries. Its 1990 nominal growth rate was only 0.1% in Czechoslovakia, 28.7% in Hungary and 157.9% in Poland. The same figures for 1991 are respectively 26.7%, 28.6% and 45% and for 1992, 23% in the Czech Republic, 4.6% in Slovakia, 27.3% in Hungary, 43.1% in Poland and 131.5% in Slovenia, while for 1993, 17.9%, 16.4%, 19.8% (at the end of September of 1992 and 1993), 35% and 64.7%, respectively.

Money supply data compared to consumer price increase level show a somewhat different picture: real money contracted over 1990 and 1991, but this tendency did not

18

continue everywhere in 1992. A decrease in real money supply was especially strong in the first year of the stabilization programmes, namely, in Poland in 1990 and 1991, in Czechoslovakia in 1991, in former Yugoslavia in 1990 and in Slovenia in 1992. Cumulative real money stock decrease was most dramatic in Poland between 1990 and 1992, then in Czechoslovakia and finally in Hungary. In some countries, 1992 was a turning point, in others monetary restraint continued. Drastic decrease in real money continued in Slovakia and Slovenia, there was a moderate growth in Hungary and a sizeable real money expansion in the Czech Republic and Poland.

For the whole of 1993, restrictiveness measured by real money expanded again in some countries (the Czech Republic, Hungary, Slovakia), in Poland real money supply did not change significantly, while in Slovenia it became expansive. Since real GDP has fallen in all the countries considered, the size of monetary restriction has become smaller, but is still substantial.

Domestic credit expansion has been the main source of money creation everywhere. Foreign assets have had considerable effects as well, whereas foreign currency deposits have constituted a substantial share of the total money supply, although varying from country to country (see Table 2).

Table 2
Nominal credit changes between 1990 and 1993 (%)

	1990	1991	1992	1993
Czech Republic	–	–	16.8	17.1
Hungary[1]	11.1	7.2	10.2	17.2
Poland[1]	249.4	97.4	90.8	51.3
Slovakia	–	–	20.3	13.0
Slovenia	–	–	91.3	116.0
Czechoslovakia	11.1	7.1	–	–
Former Yugoslavia	429.0	165.6		–

[1] 1993 data: growth rate between September 1992 and September 1993.

Source: National Statistics; *European Economic Survey*, UN, various years; *The Vienna Institute Monthly Report*, 1993, No. 31.

The structure of credit expansion also differed from country to country. Generally, in Poland and Hungary the share of domestic credit used by the governments has been much larger than in Czechoslovakia. Credits to the corporate sector and households have been smaller in the two former countries.

In 1993 domestic credits were still the main source of money supply growth in the Czech Republic, although the growth rate of foreign resource inflow at the beginning of the year was much faster than the growth of domestic credit for the year as a whole. The growth in domestic credit was determined by the growth of credits to companies and individuals (+88 billion CKR, i.e. Czech crown), while the net indebtedness of the government with the banking sector decreased (–28.8 billion CKR).

In Slovakia, broad money declined in the first two months of 1993 and it reached its end-1992 level only by May. In the growth of broad money, a particular role was played by the growth of foreign currency deposits. Although credit expansion in real terms was negative, much of its nominal growth was due to the sizeable and ever growing fiscal deficit which had to be financed by the central bank and the commercial banks.

In Hungary, the structure of money supply growth since 1991 has been worsening. While the share of foreign assets has declined, the share of credits has increased. In 1992, within the credits, more than 70% of the growth of broad money and treasury bill stock was emanated from the financing needs of the state budget. This tendency continued in 1993. By 1993, just as in the Czech Republic, the difference between money supply and credit growth became much narrower.

In Poland, the situation has been very similar in some respects. However, as opposed to Czechoslovakia and Hungary, here the credit expansion has been faster than the money supply growth, and there has been real credit growth since 1991. In 1993 (until September), the main cause of money supply growth was the growth of net indebtedness of the budgetary sector, sharing up to 84.9%, although its importance decreased in the course of the year.

In Slovenia, 1993 was the year when domestic assets showed very fast growth, faster than the money supply. There was an increase even in real terms. Within that, especially claims of the central bank on the government grew fast.

Except for Poland (and Slovenia in 1993), nominal credit expansion had generally been slower than the growth of money supply, which partially reflects the fact that foreign assets accounted for the money supply growth in an increasing share; however, by 1993, the difference between their growth rate became much smaller.

As it seems, worsening budgetary positions gradually shifted credit allocation from the corporate sector, with all its economic consequences, hardening credit conditions for the non-government sector, which in turn negatively affected economic activity. The financing needs of budget deficits put the interest rates under pressure as well.

Instruments of monetary control

Indirect tools of monetary policy gradually gained importance relative to the more direct ones in the Visegrád countries and Slovenia, although the direct tools continued dominating policy implementation.

Interests and the exchange rate have remained the major policy tools of all Visegrád countries' central banks as well as of the Slovenian one. Nominal interest rates have generally been high. The exchange rate after the initial devaluation became undervalued, but later on, by playing a decisive role in bringing down inflation, the undervalued position gradually ceased.

Although the central banks usually intended to maintain positive interest rates, in practice real interest rates were often negative, especially during accelerating inflation rate values.

In 1990, no money market existed yet in Czechoslovakia. Monetary control used first of all direct instruments. After 1992, significant changes were gradually introduced, although the money market is still in its infancy. In 1990, monetary policy targets were secured by an administratively set refinancing credit interest rate. In 1991, also other administrative measures, such as direct credit volume and interest rate ceilings, were applied, which then became gradually eliminated in 1992, although they were partially substituted by the so-called window guidance of the central bank.

Refinancing auctions have been used since April 1991, lombard credits since mid-1991 and daily auctions for refinancing credit since late 1991.

Since the stock of bonds on the market has been negligible, reserve requirements and discount rate policy have remained the major tools. Discount rate policy started to be actively used from the beginning of the transition period, and its impact on the interest rate level has lost its importance in the course of time. In late 1992, auctions in refinancing credit became a major source of bank refinancing.

After the dissolution of the Czechoslovak monetary union, the National Bank of Slovakia retained most of the institutional arrangements that were valid for the former State Bank of Czechoslovakia. Most of the policy tools of the former Czechoslovak central bank remained in effect in Slovakia too. The capacity of the Slovak monetary authorities and the underdeveloped money markets did not allow further steps in advancing more indirect monetary management. From January 1, 1993, the National Bank of Slovakia reintroduced credit ceilings.

The National Bank of Hungary has been using traditional central bank tools in implementing its policy (refinancing, reserve requirements, open market operations and interbank money market) since the late 1980s. Its set of tools, however, has undergone substantial changes.

Administrative control on company deposits was abolished and lending interest rates were made free already in 1987. Interest rate ceilings on household deposits and loans ceased in the course of 1991 and early 1992. In fact, the development of deposit and lending interest rates has been determined by market supply and demand since 1991.

The share of refinancing activities and administrative reallocation of savings by the central bank tended to decrease (by the end of 1992 about 40% of commercial bank lending was financed by the central bank), and in its allocation mechanism, market conform instruments, such as auctions, have been used increasingly. An important element in the process of improvement of instruments has been the unification of the reserve requirements. A new element in the set of implementation of monetary policy in 1992 was the creation of an interbank foreign exchange market.

In Poland, restrictive and cautious monetary policy was pursued, which was helped during the second half of 1990, besides interest and the exchange rate, obligatory reserve requirements and open market operations, also by an additional administrative tool: the credit ceilings.

The importance of using the different instruments has changed over time. From the second half of 1990, administrative control played perhaps the most significant role and was in effect until the end of 1992. Open market operations (sales and purchase of treasury bills) started in 1990 and then gained increasing importance. Reserve requirements have been used since 1989. Refinancing credit (which is used on a case-by-case basis) and interest rates have been gradually decreasing since 1991.

The Bank of Slovenia originally operated within the former Yugoslav federal monetary system. After gaining independence, the country inherited the former Yugoslav two-tier banking system. Later, the Bank of Slovenia was given full independence and it had to phase out many of its previous traditional instruments of monetary control, such as selective loans, administrative controls on lending and rediscount facilities.

The role of obligatory reserves has decreased. In complementing monetary policy, the main instruments have been: three types of central bank bills, liquidity loans, lombard loans, repurchase agreements, foreign exchange interventions, and an administrative instrument, namely, the foreign exchange minimum.

Although central bank policies during the first few years of transformation in the Visegrád countries and Slovenia intended to be restrictive, their efficiency was reduced by inter-company indebtedness and the underdevelopment and poor capital adequacy of the banking system.

Notes on the policy implementation
of individual countries

In Czechoslovakia, the 1990 scenario of economic reform envisaged restrictive monetary and credit policies.

As nominal money supply was considered a nominal anchor of the stabilization process and it was thought to be determined basically through domestic credit growth, the intermediate target of 1990 was the growth rate of domestic credit, which prescribed virtual stagnation in nominal terms. In fact, nominal domestic credits grew by almost 10% in 1990, due first of all to the increase of the credit to government, caused by currency devaluation effects.

For 1991, monetary policy was again formulated as restrictive, however, no intermediate target was set different from the one in the previous year. In the first half of 1991, monetary restraint continued in order to prevent a price jump. In the second half of the year, having seen that inflation was under control, monetary policy was slightly eased. At an annual level, while domestic credit grew by 7.1%, money supply grew by about 27%, compared to a price increase of more than 50%. This is considered to be an extraordinarily sharp restriction.

Within the credit growth, credit to government substantially decreased, while credits to companies showed a slight increase in nominal terms.

For 1992, a neutral monetary policy was designed thanks to favourable developments in inflation and external factors: broad money was planned to grow by 19.5%. The growth of broad money supply (definition M_2) actually exceeded the growth rate projected (it was about 25%), due to a balance of payment surplus and loans related to privatization.

From the middle of 1992, monetary policy was complicated by speculations related to the eventual split of the Czechoslovak state and monetary union, and to the implementation of a new tax system, which led to a cautious and slightly restrictive monetary policy at the beginning of 1993.

After the rapid and smooth currency split, the Czech National Bank eased its monetary policy from the second quarter of 1993. Money supply, after a gradual decline at the beginning of the year, recovered from the second quarter and so did domestic credit.

In Slovakia, monetary policy in 1992 was much tighter than in the whole of the Czechoslovak Federation. Against the 17% broad money supply in the whole of the Federation, it was only 4.5% in Slovakia, which partly reflects weaker economic activities and also capital flight due to speculations. At the same time, domestic credit growth was substantial, mainly due to increasing credits to government. At the end of the year, a more restrictive federal monetary policy was particularly dramatic in Slovakia, that cut back credit growth.

In 1993, after the dissolution of the Federation and the currency union, the Slovak central bank continued to apply tight monetary conditions to defend its new currency and to reach a low inflation target. The beginning of the year experienced a nominal decrease of the broad money supply, mainly due to the decrease in foreign exchange reserves. From the second quarter, however, the growth rate became positive again. Credit conditions were tight during the first half of 1993, declining in real terms, and a substantial part was due to fiscal deficit.

The 1991 policy objectives of the National Bank of Hungary were the maintenance of international solvency, improvement of the external position, and the prevention of the acceleration of inflation. In that year the National Bank of Hungary adjusted its target for the increase of money supply, 24–26%, to the expected nominal growth rate of the GDP.

The National Bank of Hungary pursued a slightly restrictive monetary policy, concentrating on banks' liquidity, in order to keep the growth rate of domestic credit within the limits projected. Despite the restrained credit policy, due to surplus of current account and inflow of foreign investments, it was very difficult to keep money supply within the targeted range. Money supply grew by 24.5%, while GDP grew only by 10.7% in nominal terms. Net domestic credit grew by much less than the money supply. The only item limiting money supply was the fall in credit to households, whereas the budget deficit and the improvement in the external position increased the money supply considerably.

The central bank targeted neither money supply nor domestic credit growth for 1992. It rather concentrated on endeavouring the decrease of interest rates and the deceleration of the inflation rate; this was thought to be achieved by avoiding real depreciation of the domestic currency.

While at the beginning of 1992 the central bank implemented a cautious policy, from the second quarter it became less restrictive, which continued until the third quarter when it turned out that year-end inflation would be higher than expected. From that time on, the central bank became more cautious again.

Generally, the central bank was only partially cutting the banking systems' liquidity in 1992. It was limiting the short-term refinancing credit, but was not increasing the obligatory reserve ratio. Also an open market operation was used to a very limited extent in order to decrease the bank's liquidity.

Broad money grew by 27% in 1992, exceeding the growth rate of the nominal GDP. Larger money demand was caused first of all by structural changes in the economy (growth of the number of market agents, strengthening of liquidity constraint in the economy, etc.). Net domestic credit grew by 103%, as projected, however, its structure was much worse than previously projected: almost the total of the credit growth was caused by the state budget deficit.

Among the factors of money supply growth, the most important element was again the net borrowing requirement of the state budget, which increased by HUF 263.7 billion (within which the effects of the 1992 credit consolidation are extremely important). Another very important factor was net foreign assets, which represented an amount of HUF 76 billion and there was a HUF 86 billion increase in other assets of the banking system (which included bad debts as well).

In Poland, the central bank directly determines the stock of high-powered money, while elements of broad money are indirectly influenced by the market interest rate, interest rate on refinancing credit and bank reserves. In 1990 and 1992, actual levels of money supply substantially exceeded the nominal money targets of the Polish central bank. This was caused by an unexpected current account surplus and a credit expansion to the corporate sector in 1990, while it was mostly due to the growth of net foreign reserves in 1992. In 1991, the actual money expansion did not differ significantly from the level targeted. On the other hand, the actual structure of the sources of money supply growth differed from the one planned. In the period considered, Polish monetary policy was extremely restrictive, especially from 1990 until 1992. However, it was only in 1991 that nominal money supply was effectively controlled.

Monetary policy in the independent Slovenia was determined by a hyper-inflation and by the fact that the country had no initial foreign exchange reserves. The primary objective in late 1991 was to bring down banks' global liquidity and neutralize their excess liquidity. Another objective was to reduce the level of the banks' obligatory reserves.

In the first months after monetary independence, the Bank of Slovenia successfully drained the excess liquidity with an initial reduction of the money supply.

Monetary policy since then has been aimed at regulating the quantity of money in circulation, with the Bank of Slovenia targeting directly the quantity of high-powered money. The exchange rate and the secondary goal (i.e. the increase of high-powered money) were monitored and supported by individual measures. Due to extraordinary circumstances which are understandable in a newly independent state, the time horizon of the Bank of Slovenia had to be very limited and had a monthly rather than a yearly character. Its sound anti-inflationary preference, however, was explicit.

From October 1991 till February 1992, the money growth had to be cut back. The initial tightening of monetary policy succeeded in reducing the growth of monetary aggregates and reduced price and wage inflation (except in December). In December of 1991, monetary policy was further tightened because of the high seasonal increase in basic money supply (definition M_1). Initial monetary adjustment in Slovenia, as detailed above, lasted until February 1992. Real demand for money was stable in the rest of 1992.

In 1992 and 1993, monetary policy was concentrated on reducing inflation and inflationary expectations. Monetary policy in 1992 was regulating the quantity of money in circulation, targeting directly the growth of high-powered money. Its instruments aimed at the maintenance of the general liquidity of banks and especially the liquidity of banks in foreign payments. The exchange rate was monitored and supported by individual measures.

From March to around mid-1992, the Bank of Slovenia gradually adjusted money supply to the accelerating rate of inflation and falling velocity of circulation. In the second half of the year, monetary policy was relaxed, as inflation came down. The monetary policy intended to reduce the interest rates and to manage the exchange rate. In order to achieve this objective, the central bank allowed a real growth in the money supply by a more relaxed monetary policy, which in fact resulted in the reduction of the interest rates in the money markets from 30% at the beginning of 1992 to 11% by mid-1993. From mid-1992, monetary policy stabilized and changed: the quantity of central bank money became much smaller than before. However, in the last quarter of the year, the quantity of money increased more markedly as a result of growth in real transactions.

Recent inflationary developments

In the analysed economies, there was a generally improved inflation performance also in 1994, as inflation continued to decline further, albeit at a much lower speed. This was in sharp contrast with the success in beating inflation in Croatia or Yugoslavia, where inflation was virtually stopped by the radical measures after a long period of hyper-inflation, or in Romania where it was reduced from three digit to medium level. In the East-Central European economies, inflation declined only in the Czech Republic and Slovakia. However, the underlying inflation did not grow smaller in these two economies either, which becomes clear if we subtract from the inflation record of 1993 the one-time price increase caused by the introduction of the value added tax.

Contrary to these two economies, inflation did not decline substantially in Poland and Hungary, where it remained at moderate levels.

Behind the general picture, there were interesting structural changes in the different indicators of inflation. First, the decline of producer price indices was stronger than that of consumer prices. This was due to the more rapid increase of service prices (which was in accordance with the changes in domestic consumption demand and the growth of the tertiary sector), the strong disciplinary impact of the exchange rate policies – except Hungary (where both the fixed and the forward looking crawling peg exchange regimes put an upward ceiling for the price increases in the sectors of tradables) and finally to the changes in the internal terms of trade in favour of agriculture, which was reflected in the growth of agricultural prices.

Secondly, the wage inflation in 1994 was weaker than a year earlier, but the increase of real wages and real product wages exceeded the levels of 1993. Therefore, labour cost pressures were stronger in 1994 than in 1993 and this put an upward pressure on price increases. The increase of real product wages was stimulated by growing domestic demand, sometimes also by expansive fiscal policies which allowed bigger wage increases in both state and private enterprises.

In Hungary, inflation in 1994 remained at the level of 1993 on a yearly basis, but the monthly changes showed a steadily increasing trend. The main driving factors behind the inflation were tax changes (increase of value added and consumption taxes, which had a strong inflationary pressure), strong nominal devaluation of the currency as a result of the change in exchange rate policy from maintaining a stable real exchange rate to real exchange depreciation, a significant increase in agricultural prices, high nominal and real wage increases. Besides all these, the inflationary expectations further accelerated as the credibility of economic policy was weakening and the macroeconomic imbalances were growing. The deteriorating macroeconomic performance was reflected in slowly growing monthly price changes, which led to a much stronger inflation in 1995.

The driving factors behind the inflation in Poland were mainly supply-side and inertial elements. The most important among them were: the high real wage growth, the increase in administrative prices (especially of energy) and the built-in inflationary impact of the crawling peg exchange rate policy. The crawling peg regime established a minimal benchmark for the price increases which had a strong inflationary impact in the sectors of both tradables and non-tradables. Besides that, inflationary expectations increased in 1994 as the country started to experience strong capital inflows which were due to the difference between domestic and international returns. The direct consequences of capi-

25

tal inflows were not yet felt in 1994, but they put increasing pressure on money supply and reduced the efficiency and credibility of the anti-inflationary policy.

Contrary to Poland, the capital inflows did not have an inflationary impact in 1994 in the Czech Republic which experienced a steady decline in inflation compared to 1993, although the underlying inflation remained almost equal to that of 1993. In the Czech Republic, the most important factor of the successful reduction of inflation was the maintenance of the fixed exchange rate regime and of stable monetary policy. The reputation of monetary authorities was good and this helped much in reducing actual and expected inflation. At the same time, in 1994 there were also some factors which may in the longer term contribute to increased inflationary pressures. First, the growth of nominal wages far exceeded productivity gains and this led to increasing real wages which were not moderated later. Secondly, the inflow of foreign capital and the worsening trade balance increased doubts about the sustainability of fixed exchange rate, which may lead to devaluation and thus to the loss of the most important – and after the relaxation of incomes policies, the final – anchor of the stabilization policy. Therefore, the low level of inflation may be endangered already in the short term and there may be much more significant price changes.

In Slovenia, the 1993 inflation almost halved in 1994 and reached the second lowest level after the Czech Republic in the region. The main reasons for the declining inflation were the increased stability of the national currency, the high credibility of the macroeconomic policies and the much lower nominal wage increases than in 1993. These factors supported the continued decline of price increases, which has been observable since the introduction of the radical stabilization measures and the new currency in 1991. The only concern is the monetary impact of the currency inflows which led to a rapid increase in money supply. So far this increase has been balanced by the growth in money demand due to the high spreads between international and domestic interest rates. But the persistence of capital inflows may lead to renewed inflationary pressures or may require strong sterilization measures by the monetary authorities.

To sum up: the countries in the region may be divided into two groups. To the first one belong those (the Czech Republic, Slovenia and to a lesser extent Slovakia) which were able to maintain balanced budgets, credible macroeconomic policies and stable nominal or real exchange rates, and this supported the decline of price increases to almost a one digit level. On the other hand, the two other economies (Hungary and Poland) were less able to curb inflationary pressures, due to more relaxed macroeconomic policies and/or supply-side and inertial factors of inflation.

Bibliography

Blanchard, O. – Dornbusch, R. – Krugman, P. – Layard, R. – Summers, R. (1991): *Economic Reform in Eastern Europe*. MIT Press.
Brada, J. (1992): Is There a J-curve for the Economic Transition from Socialism to Capitalism? *Economics of Planning*, 1992/1.
Bruno, M. (1993): Stabilization and the Macroeconomics of Transition – How Different is Eastern Europe? *Economics of Transition*, 1993/1.
Commander, S. (1991): *Managing Inflation in the Socialist Economies in Transition*. The World Bank.
Dewatripont, R. (1992): The Virtues of Gradualism and Legitimacy in the Transition to the Market Economy. *Economic Journal*, 1992/March.

Ellman, J. – Gaidar, J. – Kolodko, G. (1992): *Economic Transition in Eastern Europe.* Cambridge, Massachusetts.

Funke, N. (1993): The Role of Credibility of Government Policy: Lessons for Economies in Transition. *Intereconomics,* 1993/3.

Kolodko, G. (1992): *Hyperinflation and Stabilization in Post-socialist Economies.* Kluwer, Boston.

McKinnon, R. (1991): *The Order of Economic Liberalization: Financial Control in the Transition to Market Economy.* The Johns Hopkins University Press, Baltimore.

Rybczynski, T. (1991): The Sequencing of Reform? *Oxford Review of Economic Policy,* 1991/4.

Williamson, J. (1991): *The Economic Opening of Eastern Europe.* Institute for International Economics, Washington.

Exchange rate policies in economies in transition

PÁL GÁSPÁR

Introduction

During the transition, exchange rate policies play an important role both in reducing macroeconomic imbalances accompanying stabilization and in promoting structural changes. Exchange rate policies are important in short-term macroeconomic stabilization, as they determine both the speed of disinflation and the real costs of stabilization. On the other hand, exchange rate policies influence the speed, the sequencing and the macroeconomic consequences as well as the sustainability of the liberalization process and the opening up of the economies. Finally, they influence the structural shifts in the economies and also the flexibility of structural adjustments. Among these shifts, the most important one is related to the change in the relative importance of the sectors of tradables and non-tradables.

The last four years of transition provide a good opportunity to make a comparative study on the exchange rate policies applied by the East-Central European economies. It may give us an insight into the common features of the economies in transition as well as the country-specific ones as regards exchange rate policy, and can help in identifying the major successes and problems.

This chapter tries to evaluate the differing exchange rate arrangements, the similar developments and the required adjustments in the applied exchange rate policies. First it examines briefly some of the most important proposals for exchange rate policy in economies in transition. Then it describes the country experiences accumulated so far. Finally, it deals with the similar and the different features of the exchange rate developments in the East-Central European economies.

Views on exchange rate policies in East-Central Europe

As exchange rate policies are crucial in the economies in transition, the literature is abundant regarding suggestions for the exchange rate policies to be applied by them. At the outset there was a relatively general consensus regarding the application of fixed (or pegged) exchange rates in the initial stages of macroeconomic stabilization and liberalization. Many arguments supported the use of fixed exchange rates.

First, the traditional discipline argument (Willett et al. 1993) was mentioned as an advantage of the fixed exchange rates over flexible ones in a period of highly unstable and varying inflation and price liberalization. According to this argument, the use of fixed exchange rates reduces the inflationary pressures by keeping the growth of the nominal variables (i.e. prices, wages, interest rates) under control. As the growth of prices and nominal wages during the transition was expected to be volatile and strong, it was assumed that the control effect of fixed exchange rates could have useful impacts on the speed and costs of stabilization.

This traditional discipline effect of the fixed exchange rates was further strengthened by the experiences of the developing countries using the exchange rate as nominal anchors to disinflate in the 1980s. The successful disinflation policies of Israel (1985–1987), Argentina (1991–1992) and the successes in the earlier stage of the heterodox stabilization programmes (Argentina in 1985–1986, Brazil in 1986–1987) in combating inflation raised hopes that the exchange rate policy as a nominal anchor would have a strong deflationary impact.

Besides these empirical examples, it was further assumed that by using the exchange rate as a nominal anchor, deflation would be less costly as the expectations and later the growth of nominal variables would converge rather rapidly to the level consistent with lower inflation. As the stabilization of the initial corrective inflation required the use of some forms of anchor, the adoption of the exchange rate as an anchor seemed to be superior to the use of money supply. The exchange rate was a more visible anchor; due to strong inflationary expectations, it had a bigger impact on the development of nominal variables, and was less dependent.

Second, it was thought in line with the "one price theory" that by applying fixed exchange rates together with the liberalization of imports and the reduction of administrative regulations, the domestic prices in the economies in transition would rapidly converge to the international ones. By adopting fixed exchange rate regimes, the countries would enjoy both the micro- and the macroeconomic discipline effects that the opening up of their markets might exert on their domestic economy.

The final argument proposed for the use of a fixed exchange rate is related to the modern idea of the credibility impact. By reducing the possibility of using surprise inflation to combat the domestic macroeconomic imbalances and by tying the hands of monetary policy, it was assumed that the fixed exchange rate regime could increase both the credibility of and the commitment to an anti-inflationary policy irrespective of its costs. This argument was put forward in justifying both the strong versions of the fixed exchange rate policies which imply the use of a currency board and the weaker forms which have a one-sided commitment to maintain a pegged exchange rate.

Simultaneously with these arguments in favour of fixed exchange rates, the counter-arguments have also been widespread. First, regarding the credibility impact of the fixed exchange rates in the economies in transition, it was mentioned that generally – and particularly in the case of the EMS (European Monetary System) – it was not the credibility of tying the hands of the monetary policy which reduced the inflation, but instead, the anti-inflationary macroeconomic policies increased the credibility of the applied exchange rate policies. If the underlying policies are not consistent with the exchange rate policy, then the credibility impact is not valid and there is less scope for adjustment under fixed exchange rates.

Second, the use of pegged exchange rates in the economies in transition generally does not mean an irrevocable fix, but only a temporary one, as it is well known already at the beginning of economic programmes that subsequent devaluations would be necessary. Therefore, the assumed strong anti-inflationary credibility impact is not operating, as the public is expecting subsequent devaluations.

Besides that, the anti-inflationary impact of the fixed exchange rates is also weakened by the necessity of a strong devaluation at the outset of the programme. In order to avoid the later overvaluation of the currency and the reversal of trade liberalization, it was suggested to begin the programme with a strong devaluation, followed by fixing at this depreciated level. But this exchange rate behaviour would harmfully affect the expectations and would contribute to fuelling inflation from the supply side.

Third, the assumed positive outcomes of rapid disinflation through the use of fixed exchange rate as the nominal anchor were dismissed on two grounds. On the one hand, the experience of the developing countries has shown that these gains are only short-term and temporary, and later the costs of exchange rate appreciation relating to output might outweigh them. On the other hand, as the markets for factors of production are inflexible in these economies, even the gains may be eroded due to this inflexibility. The presence of price and wage rigidities may induce inertial inflation which is in general incompatible with the use of fixed exchange rates.

Finally, as the inflation–unemployment trade-off is flatter in the case of fixed exchange rates, the governments are more tempted to use surprise inflation to combat the macroeconomic problems. This is even more so in these economies, as they face simultaneous disequilibria, while at the same time the macroeconomic policies are even more time-inconsistent.

Considering this criticism of the fixed or pegged exchange rate regimes, flexible exchange rates were suggested. Among their advantages, the most commonly mentioned one was the unnecessity of determining the equilibrium exchange rate which has to be fixed. As the factors affecting the evolution of the exchange rate[1] change rapidly in these economies, the equilibrium exchange rate is also varying rapidly, and therefore, it cannot be fixed at the beginning. If it is fixed at wrong levels, the direct impact both on the macroeconomic aggregates and on the expectations would cause significant costs for the economies in question.

Second, it is important for the sustainability of the pegged exchange rates to have relatively small changes in the value of the currency to which it is pegged and in the conditions affecting the evolution of the equilibrium real exchange rate. But this is not very easy in economies in transition, and therefore these changes may have a negative impact on stabilization.

Finally, by applying flexible exchange rates, the countries may avoid resorting to administrative regulations of foreign trade in order to reverse the original steps in their import liberalization. As the foreign exchange gap may always be closed by allowing the exchange rate to adjust, the liberalized trade regime may be maintained with its favourable efficiency and macroeconomic consequences.

There were two counter-arguments raised at the beginning against the use of flexible exchange rates. First, it can frequently have a destabilizing impact on the inflationary and devaluation expectations and may move the market exchange rate in an unintended direction. The freely and – due to institutional backwardness and rudimentary market mechanisms – in wide band floating exchange rate may heavily fuel inflation and interest rates. Besides, the destabilizing speculations may impede the credibility and consistency of the stabilization and exchange rate policies. Second, well-developed and mature institutions are required to manage the flexible exchange rates. As the money

---

[1] The most important factors in these economies are: the opening up of the economies and the liberalization of factor markets, the initial monetary overhang and the later price developments, and the structural changes.

markets are underdeveloped, the instruments are not sophisticated, and the supply and demand conditions are unstable, the destabilizing speculations may be even higher than in the developed economies, which might bring unsustainable and dangerous fluctuations in the nominal and real exchange rates.

Basing our arguments on the application of the optimum currency area approach, we would expect these countries to have relatively similar exchange rate policies. As they have basically equal initial conditions, relatively similar structural and macroeconomic characteristics, there was no reason to expect significant differences in the exchange rate policies. However, the real differences both in the chosen exchange rate policy and in its impact are enormous, and not only within the region with countries of slightly different features, but also between countries with identical features (such as Latvia using flexible exchange rates and Estonia committing itself to the currency board approach).

The case of fixed exchange rates: the Czech Republic

The Czech Republic was one of the economies in the region to follow the typical way of deep devaluation with exchange rate pegging policies. Before the deep liberalization of prices and imports began in 1991, the domestic currency had been devalued in three steps, leading to about double the nominal exchange rate and about a 35% increase in the real effective exchange rate measured by both producer and consumer prices. After this sharp devaluation, the crown was fixed in January 1991 against a basket of foreign currencies roughly representing the currency composition of Czechoslovak foreign trade.

The adoption of the one-sided peg could be explained on the following grounds. First, as the Czech Republic had the tradition of sound macroeconomic policies and there was no fear of a sharp increase in inflation, there was no need to apply the Estonian currency board type fixed exchange rate policy. The fixed exchange rate could be maintained by simply following a rather conservative monetary policy, instead of determining exogenously the growth of the money supply. As the Czech National Bank tried to follow a Bundesbank-type monetary policy, no unfavourable development of the macroeconomic variables and of expectations could hurt the adoption of the peg.

Second, the original devaluation of the currency[2] was assumed to be enough to maintain a relatively stable nominal exchange rate in spite of the foreseen sizeable price increases due to the devaluation and the price liberalization. Although it was obvious that the fixed exchange rate was not an equilibrium one, it was hoped that the price increases would be temporary and would not generate, in the presence of consistent monetary policies, permanent inflationary pressures.

Third, in order to maintain the stability and achieve the trade policy and inflation goals of the exchange rate, besides the exchange rate there was also another anchor introduced, namely: wage restrictions. The Czech Republic followed a tax-based wage policy,[3] where wage increases over the allowed nominal level were punished by pro-

---

[2] In 1990 the crown was devalued in three steps by about 100%.

[3] The wage anchor had a positive impact on the exchange rate developments only in 1991 and 1992. Later it was relaxed and not followed by the companies, and this led to significant increases in the real wages and incomes after 1993.

32

hibitive taxes (this meant initially declining real wages). This second anchor significantly enhanced both the credibility of the exchange rate policy and the likeliness of maintaining the fixed exchange rate.

Finally, it was assumed by Czech experts that the maintenance of the fixed exchange rate would significantly increase the credibility of the monetary stabilization. This was due to the fact that in the case of fixed exchange rate, the hands of the central bank are tied and the growth of the domestic money supply is dependent on the monetary policy of the country to which the domestic currency is pegged. This pegging was assumed to enhance further the anti-inflationary commitment of the Czech National Bank.

Considering the last four years, the choice of the above-described exchange rate regime seems to be justified by the macroeconomic developments. On the one hand, the exchange rate and monetary policies were successful in disinflating and providing the monetary stability essential for the success of the microeconomic and structural reforms. On the other hand, the stability of the nominal exchange rate was maintained and there was no need for exchange rate adjustments. In this period, there was only one case when there were high speculations against the crown. This was during the split of the country, but the strong devaluation expectations were cooled down by the National Bank defending the already established rate. During this period, there was only one significant change in the exchange rate policy when the original basket consisting of five currencies was replaced on May 3, 1993 by a basket comprising DEM with a 65% and USD with a 35% weight.

What were the factors explaining the success in maintaining the fixed exchange rate and the absence of adjustment? The most significant one was the consistency between the exchange rate and other macroeconomic policies, particularly the monetary and the fiscal ones. Due to its balanced macroeconomic policies and the impact of certain favourable special factors,[4] the country enjoyed a gradually declining inflation and relative stability with respect to the changes in the nominal variables. In respect of monetary policy, the independence of the National Bank in formulating both its monetary and its exchange rate policy objective is worth mentioning. This independence can partly be explained by the lack of need to monetize the fiscal deficit, as the deficit was kept low.

Another factor that explains the sustainability of the fixed exchange rate was the impact of the initially strong restrictions on the capital account. Compared to Poland and Hungary, the Czech Republic maintained stricter capital controls, as these were essential to maintain the fixed exchange rate. The need to maintain strict capital controls is explained by the experience of developed market economies in the EMS, where fixed exchange rates, dependent monetary policies and capital account liberalization were not compatible. Besides that, although there is full internal convertibility for the corporate sector, the crown is not convertible for the household sector. The favourable balance of payments developments have also contributed to the stability of the exchange rate regime. Initially, the basically stable trade balance was accompanied by increasing service revenues due to the rapid development of the service sector. Later, as the competitiveness of the sector of tradables declined, the trade deficit started to worsen, which was not balanced by service receipts. At the same time, capital inflows started to grow significantly, reflecting the impact of privatization and the difference between domestic

---

[4] One special factor is the role of the split of the country in supporting the fiscal stabilization, as the Czech Republic could reduce the inter-republican transfers and the expenditures associated with it.

and international interest rates; it was also stimulated by the promise of maintaining a stable nominal exchange rate. This led to significant capital inflows far outweighing the current account deficit and contributing both to the rapid build-up of international reserves and the stability of the nominal exchange rate.

What are the problems of the Czech exchange rate policy? First, the followed practice of devaluation with fixed exchange rate policy had unfavourable consequences with respect to the structural changes in the economy. The initial devaluations moved the factors of production towards sectors with low value added (Hrnčíř 1994), while the later appreciation reduced both the competitiveness and the profitability of exports. The latter one is clearly seen in the rapid increase in the amount of inter-company payment arrears, amounting to 30% of the credits extended by the banking system towards the corporate sector. The lack of sufficient structural changes is partly responsible for the slow growth of exports after 1993, although the external demand conditions have become much more favourable than before. One of the most serious problems is obviously the significant real exchange rate appreciation that has taken place since January 1991. According to estimates, the real effective exchange rate has suffered a 35–40% appreciation if we use both the CPI (Consumer Price Index) and the PPI (Producer Price Index) as deflators. Although the initial steep depreciation gave significant room for real exchange rate adjustment, the inflationary differences rapidly eroded the competitiveness gains of the initial devaluation. This appreciation was absorbed without significant impact as long as the trade balance was not negative and the market participants were not expecting higher inflation. However, as the trade balance may deteriorate, reflecting the decline in competitiveness due to high and increasing real wages and unit labour costs, and the inflation may stabilize at a higher level than that of the major trading partners, the National Bank will be less able to maintain the fixed exchange rate.

A related issue is how the fixed exchange rate may be sustained in the light of increasing capital inflows and the pressure they are exerting on the real exchange rate. Starting from 1993, the capital account improved sharply,[5] reflecting basically the significant inflow of foreign portfolio investments and other short-term capital. This inflow contributed to the further appreciation of the real exchange rate, a phenomenon quite frequently observed in developing economies which experience large capital inflows or open their capital account.

The capital inflows created serious problems for both monetary and exchange rate policies. In order to preserve the stability of monetary aggregates, the central bank opted for sterilizing inflows, by selling – due to the lack of developed market of government bonds – own bills. This sterilization has so far been able to protect the money supply from a sharp increase, but stimulated further capital inflows, as the differences between international returns and the central bank bills were significant. The extent of capital inflow was huge compared to the domestic monetary aggregates, and this further appreciated the real exchange rate.

It is extremely difficult to determine what exchange rate policy should be followed in the light of capital inflows and the simultaneous rapidly worsening current account. One option would be to further revalue the currency in order to reduce the profitability

---

[5] The capital account changed from –6 million USD (1992) to 2496 million USD (1993), while the portfolio investments – related to the privatization programme and increasing foreign demand for the assets on the stock exchange – grew from –35 million USD to 1062 million USD.

of capital inflows. A similar outcome may be reached by allowing the currency to float within a band, as it would increase the exchange rate uncertainty and reduce capital inflows. But this option would further lead to a real exchange and even to a nominal appreciation, which would further hurt competitiveness of the sector of tradables and worsen the current account. This outcome would be quite similar to the late-1970 experience of Southern Cone economies (Argentina, Chile, Uruguay) which faced sharply deteriorating trade and current account balances due to real exchange rate appreciation stimulated by strong capital inflows. In addition, if the appreciation is not assumed by the market to be temporary but long-term, this policy may backfire, as further capital will flow in.

Another option – which is obviously demanded by producers of tradable goods – would be to devalue the currency. This would reduce the pressure from capital inflows and could improve the competitiveness of exports. But it is very dangerous to devalue in an overheated economy where the money supply and the inflationary pressures are increasing due to other factors as well. Besides, the devaluation could lead to capital outflows even if it is assumed to be a sole step or is credibly predetermined in a crawling peg framework. In this case, devaluation could neutralize the already observed positive impacts of capital inflows.

Whatever the choice of the exchange rate policy will be, the fixed exchange rate seems to be unsustainable in the medium term and should be replaced. But this long-postponed adjustment might result in additional costs both for the economy and the credibility of the economic policy.

As the two countries had a common exchange rate policy, some words should be said about the exchange rate developments in the Slovak Republic as well. After the split, the Slovak Republic maintained for a while the hard currency approach of the Czech Republic, although it was clear that this would not hold for a long term, due to the structural and macroeconomic differences between the two countries. Compared to the Czech Republic, Slovakia had higher inflation and fiscal deficit, less anti-inflationary and independent monetary policy, and the costs of transition in terms of lost output and employment were also higher here.

In addition, the structural weakness of the country indicated that the fixed exchange rate could not be maintained, as this would lead to a rapidly worsening trade balance. The share of the sector of tradables is lower, as are the competitive and high value added producing ones, which means that exchange rate adjustments are required to improve the trade balance and to increase the competitiveness of exports.

The change in the exchange rate policy came after half a year when in July 1993 the Slovak crown was devalued by 10%. The devaluation had a positive impact on the trade balance only temporarily, as the import demand was surging again and the competitiveness of exports was not restored. This is reflected in the subsequent devaluation of the crown, and in the imposition of quantitative restrictions on imports. On the other hand, the devaluation contributed to inflation and aggravated the fiscal problems.

The basic problem of the Slovak exchange rate development is related to the stance of its macroeconomic policies. As long as the monetary and fiscal policies do not exert a disciplinary impact on the nominal variables, the devaluations will be neutralized by subsequent increases in the price level and the accompanying appreciation. On the other hand, the economic and political uncertainties make the maintenance of the current imbalanced macroeconomic policies probable, which may lead to further exchange rate policy difficulties.

The forward looking crawling peg: the case of Poland

While the initial conditions in Poland differed greatly from those prevailing in Czechoslovakia, the applied macroeconomic stabilization policies were quite similar. They consisted of a rapid liberalization of prices and imports, the introduction of strict macroeconomic stabilization policies having two anchors: the increase in nominal wages and the fixed exchange rate. Notwithstanding the similarities with the Czechoslovakian fixing, there were some differences in the exchange rate policy as well.

First, the exchange rate policy acquired an external source of stability in the form of the Stabilization Fund, which could have been used in the case of trade balance difficulties. Second, it was assumed already from the beginning that the fixed exchange rate could not be maintained for a long term and later subsequent changes would become unavoidable.

The exchange rate policy had the same short-term macroeconomic impact as in the case of Czechoslovakia. It contributed to the introduction of current account convertibility, helped in maintaining the trade liberalization and initially improved the trade balance. On the other hand, it adversely influenced inflation, the changes in the fiscal balance as well as the structural changes.

Due to the higher than expected corrective inflation and the changes in the restrictive nature of the monetary policy starting from the second half of 1990, the exchange rate became overvalued. Therefore correction of the exchange rate became unavoidable in 1991, thus the zloty was devalued in May 1991. But this devaluation could not improve the real exchange rate, as the underlying inflation rate was high due to the high fiscal deficit and the rapid increase in nominal wages.

Therefore, a different exchange rate regime had to be introduced which was the pre-announced crawling peg. By pre-announcing the rates of exchange rate depreciation, the central bank tried to influence the evolution of expectations of the market agents. Besides that, this policy had to serve a direct anti-inflationary goal, because – as in open and liberalized economies – the speed of devaluation had to determine the price increases in the sector of tradables.

The shift toward the pre-announced crawling peg occurred in October 1991, and meant initially a 1.8% devaluation of the zloty per month. The devaluation was carried out against a basket of currencies which replaced the dollar to which the zloty was initially pegged. The introduction of the crawling peg reduced the pressures on the zloty and contributed to the improvement of the real exchange rate. But as the inflation was still high[6] in both 1991 and 1992, and the 1.8% devaluation per month was not sufficient to maintain a stable real exchange rate, further devaluations were required.

Therefore, within the framework of the crawling peg regime the zloty was devalued sometimes, the first of these devaluations having occurred in February 1992. These devaluations gave new dynamics for real exchange rate developments, which were crucial with respect to the sustainability of the followed exchange rate policy.

Starting from the second half of 1993, the macroeconomic performance of the economy improved significantly. The country started to experience strong recovery from

---

[6] The high inflation is partly related to cost pressures and increasing administrative prices and partly reflects the impact of the pursued exchange rate policy.

36

thc dccp post-stabilization recession and the GDP started to increase. The recovery of the GDP was supported by a vibrant increase of exports. The export growth was already the reflection of improving real exchange rates, the increase in the productivity in the sector of tradables and the growth of investments.

The recovery of the economy was accompanied by a decline in the inflation rate which was still high in international comparison. The achieved improvement in the fiscal balance – which reduced the public sector's borrowing requirement and the associated monetary financing – was an important factor in reducing the inflationary pressures.

The recovery of production led to a favourable current account balance which together with the declining inflation mitigated the pressures on the exchange rate adjustment.

The weakening pressure from inflation and the current account was reflected in the gradually declining amount of monthly exchange rate adjustments of the central parity. The monthly devaluations within the crawling peg regime were reduced step by step from 1.8% in August 1993 to 1.2% in January 1995. Thc decline of the monthly devaluation was partly targeted at the reduction of inflationary pressures coming from the exchange rate adjustment.

At the same time, the exchange rate developments were increasingly affected by capital inflows, just as in the case of the Czech Republic. The extent of capital inflows was basically the same, but the sources were a little different. The capital inflows in Poland were partly associated with the inflow of foreign portfolio investments and other short-term capital, but they partly also reflected the increasing exports and the improving trade balance. This increased the supply of foreign exchange and produced effects similar to those in the Czech Republic.

The reaction of the central bank was also similar, as it started to accumulate reserves and sterilized the inflow of capital. The sterilization was done through government securities, as here the market for government papers is more developed than in the Czech Republic.

The capital inflows exerted a strong pressure on the exchange rate policy as well. In order to reduce speculative inflows, the central bank had to allow the revaluation of the zloty. This was achieved by widening the band to 7% in both directions around the central parity which is determined by the monthly adjustments of the crawling peg regime. The reaction of the market was immediate, as the zloty sharply appreciated, but afterwards remained stable at the newly reached point.

The implementation of the crawling peg exchange rate regime was a widely used practice in economies stabilizing high inflation with the exchange rate as an anchor. Their adoption was required in many of the developing countries where the initial real exchange rate appreciation could no longer be sustained.

The adoption of the crawling peg regime had some favourable outcomes for the Polish economy. Due to the crawling peg regime, Poland could maintain the most stable real exchange rate among all the economies in transition. Measured by both the consumer and the producer price index, a remarkable stability can be observed in a period when the factors affecting the real exchange rate varied substantially.

The adoption of the crawling peg system was an important policy decision, as it was able to support both the adjustment of the real exchange rate and the disinflation of the economy. But the sustainability of the exchange rate regime depended greatly on the macroeconomic policies. If they had not been consistent with the crawling peg, it could not have been maintained so long. In this respect, the most significant change was the reversal of the trend in the increasing fiscal deficit, which also reduced the pressure on monetary policy. While the deficit was declining, the inflation stabilized at a relatively high level, higher than in the other East-Central European economies, which caused some difficulties for the exchange rate management.

It is a deficiency of the crawling peg that it introduces a lower minimum rate of inflation related to the monthly changes in the exchange rate. This makes the correction of the underlying inflation rate more difficult than it would be in the case of other exchange rate regimes.

Besides that, as the changes in the nominal variables are connected to a certain degree with the exchange rate adjustments, their growth is also adversely affected by the crawling peg regime. On the other hand, there is a danger that if the nominal variables develop in a non-consistent way with the exchange rate adjustments, then unfavourable expectations may emerge, reducing the credibility and sustainability of the pursued exchange rate policy.

Finally, in the case of the crawling peg, the impact of the external shocks on the domestic variables might be stronger than in the case of a flexible or even a fixed exchange rate. Taking into consideration the likelihood and the intensity of these shocks, this creates an additional source of inflationary pressure in the economy.

The case of the adjustable peg: Hungary

Hungary was the only country that avoided the devaluation with fixing or free float of its exchange rate and opted instead for an adjustable peg regime from the outset. The reasons behind the lack of an initial sharp devaluation and later fixing were related to the balance of payments problems of the late 1980s, the initial rounds of price and import liberalization of 1987–1989 and the relative openness of the economy. Due to these factors, the policy of stepwise devaluations was followed and the official exchange rate was brought into line with the prevailing market exchange rate.

As regards the choice of the initial exchange rate regime, the fixed exchange rate was opposed due to the difficulty of determining the equilibrium exchange rate, to the assumption of later price increases as the new rounds of import and price liberalization would occur, and to the need of using the exchange rate policy for the improvement of the current account. The free float of the forint was also not an issue, as the capital market and the financial institutions were not mature enough to keep the fluctuation within a reasonable range without inducing destabilizing speculations.

In the case of the adjustable peg regime, the evolution of the real exchange rate is the key issue, because the trade policy and the inflationary goals of the exchange rate policy are in conflict. The exchange rate policy pursued in Hungary may be divided into four periods.

The first lasted from 1987 to 1989 and was characterized by real exchange rate appreciation. In this period the currency was pegged to a basket of currencies representing the currency composition of foreign trade. The primary goal of the exchange rate policy was to increase the competitiveness of exports and to improve the balance of payments. The exchange rate policy played an important role in influencing the outcome of import and price liberalization, as the quantitative restrictions were not replaced by tariffs.

Devaluations were frequent (nine times in 1989 alone) and sometimes significant. They helped in closing the foreign gap, but resulted in strong inflationary pressures and devaluation expectations as they were generally connected with new rounds of price and import liberalization. Thus the devaluations put the economy on a higher inflationary level and sustained the inflationary consequences of price liberalization.

In the second stage, between 1990 and 1991, the exchange rate adjustments acquired a new character. First, the policy of dispersed small devaluations was applied in order to reduce the inflationary consequences of exchange rate adjustments. It was assumed that the mini-devaluations would have less inflationary costs than the earlier bigger ones. Second, the currency was pegged against a basket consisting of the dollar and the ECU having equal shares, instead of the basket representing the currency composition of the foreign trade. Third, the objectives of the exchange rate policy became more balanced and more emphasis was put on restraining inflation. This was due to the inflationary consequences of price liberalization and the loosening stance of the monetary policy which became neutral in 1990. As the devaluations became less common and the inflation rate was increasing, the real exchange rate became more neutral, reversing the earlier trend of real exchange rate depreciation.

The next period of the exchange rate policy lasted from the first quarter of 1992 until the third quarter of 1993 and was directed at reducing the inflation. The reasons behind this choice are manifold. First, in this period the monetary (as well as the fiscal) policy was completely reversed and the money-based stabilization came to an end, that is, the money supply no longer played the role of the nominal anchor. The expansionary stance of the monetary policy was due to the intention to reduce the nominal interest rates in order to reduce the output and employment losses of the disinflation and the interest costs of deficit financing.

Secondly, the inflation goal of the exchange rate policy was intended to reduce the negative impact the inflation exerted on the fiscal balance and the current account. It was recognized that the inflation negatively affected the fiscal developments, reduced the inflow of foreign capital crucial with respect to financing the current account, and affected adversely the trade balance. Therefore, the exchange rate policy had to support the reduction of inflation, as the budget deficit grew and the monetary policy was tied to the fiscal one.

The policy of allowing the real exchange rate to appreciate was accomplished with small devaluations dispersed in time, not reaching the inflationary differences between Hungary and its major trading partners, and having only a slight impact on the inflationary expectations. In 1992 and in the first half of 1993, there were only five devaluations, all less than 3%. In the meantime, the currency basket changed in August 1993 due to the turmoil in the EMS, and the ECU was replaced by the DEM.

As this was a period of increasing inflation (which reached the lowest level in June 1992 when the CPI grew by 22.1%), the small devaluations led to exchange rate appreciation. The magnitude of this appreciation is different depending on the base we choose, on the deflator we use, since there are tremendous differences between the development of the PPI, CPI or unit labour cost indices. The CPI suggests a 20–25% appreciation of the forint in the period between 1991 and 1993, while the PPI shows only a 10% appreciation in the same period.

The policy of letting the exchange rate appreciate did not reach its final goal of reducing the inflation, as it was accelerating due to other factors. On the other hand, the trade balance has also worsened due to the impact of declining exports related to the supply-side and institutional factors.[7] Due to these changes, the exchange rate policy became under pressure of supporting both the trade balance and the targeted inflation level.

The last stage since the third quarter of 1993 is characterized by more frequent devaluations aimed at reaching a neutral real exchange rate, while the policy of small devaluations was combined with strong periodical adjustments. These big devaluations were required, according to the policy-makers, for two reasons. First, the trade balance worsened further in 1993 and 1994, and it was assumed that real exchange depreciation could improve both the competitiveness of the sector of tradables and the trade balance. On the other hand, the worsening macroeconomic indicators (especially the current account deficit reaching 9% of the GDP in both 1993 and 1994, and the fiscal deficit reaching 6–7% in the same years) produced strong speculations against the domestic currency. This had a very unfavourable impact on the level and stability of the domestic interest rates, which worsened further the trade balance, as exports were postponed, while imports were advanced, and capital flight also increased.

The first big devaluation occurred in August 1994 when the forint was devalued by 8%. Later the exchange rate policy tried to return to small devaluations, but the adjustments remained higher and more frequent than earlier. The exchange rate policy measures were not accompanied by fiscal adjustments and thus they did not improve the trade balance.

As the macroeconomic indicators did not improve at all, the speculative attacks re-emerged and this finally led to a new devaluation of 9% in March 1995. But this time the adjustment did not remain a discrete step, as the exchange rate regime was modified from adjustable peg to crawling peg, and the devaluation was accompanied by restrictive macroeconomic policies. The monthly devaluation was initially set at 1.9% per month, which is assumed to be reduced to 1.3% in the second half of the year.

The shift to crawling peg was an unavoidable step, as the adjustable peg regime fully lost its credibility. The exchange rate policy and the small devaluations were not backed by appropriate monetary and especially fiscal policy measures. The exchange rate policy lost its own anchors and thus it became increasingly incredible that the central bank would be able to continue its policy of small devaluations dispersed in time. The exchange rate policy was unable to influence the expectations which increasingly determined the exchange rate developments. Furthermore, the exchange rate adjustments in 1994 did not reduce the speculative attacks against the forint, on the contrary, the devaluations justified them. Finally, the adjustable peg could not simultaneously mitigate the inflationary expectations and improve the competitiveness of the sector of tradables.

The experience of the Hungarian exchange rate policy allows some conclusions regarding its application in an economy in transition. First, the choice of the adjustable peg was correct due to the initial state of the economic reforms, the gradual character of liberalization and the uncertainties regarding both the equilibrium real exchange rate and the future path of the monetary policy.

---

[7] The supply-side impact is due to the fall in agricultural output, while the institutional one to the impact of the bankruptcy procedures on the export performance.

Second, the Hungarian exchange rate policy shows the negative consequences of having macroeconomic policies inconsistent with the applied exchange rate regime. Neither the fiscal, nor the monetary policies were able to support the peg and contributed to strong real exchange rate variability.

Third, the Tinbergen principle of consistency between the number of targets and tools was not considered, thus putting the exchange rate policy under double fire. As the monetary anchor was lost and the foreign exchange constraint remained strong, the exchange rate policy had to be simultaneously applied for trade policy and anti-inflationary purposes.

The case of the flexible exchange rate: Slovenia

According to the arguments of the optimal currency area theory, Slovenia – as a small, relatively open economy – had to opt for the flexible exchange rate regime. Besides the theoretical considerations, there were also practical reasons for choosing the flexible exchange rate. Among them the most important one is the lack of hard currency reserves, which did not allow the central bank to maintain whatever form of fixed or pegged exchange rate. The reserves of the Bank of Slovenia were fully depleted when the flexible exchange rate policy was introduced in 1991.

In addition, it was assumed that the separation of the country from the Yugoslav Federation and the accompanying shifts in the structure of production and foreign trade would make it impossible to determine and maintain predetermined equilibrium exchange rates. This was all the more so, as the practice of fixing the dinar to the DEM in 1989 proved to be unsuccessful, partly because of the wrong original exchange rate.

After the introduction of the flexible exchange rate, the development of the exchange rate policy may be divided into two periods. In the first period, from the introduction of the flexible exchange rate in October 1991 until the second quarter of 1992, there was a sharp depreciation of the Slovenian tollar, caused by several factors.

First, the credibility of the central bank was low, as it was a new institution and the experiences with the earlier central bank commitments were not convincing.

Second, the reserves and the supply of foreign currency were small, as the country had a current account deficit not compensated by the inflow of foreign capital. Besides that, when the tollar and the flexible exchange rate were introduced, inflation was running at 22% per month. This resulted in a strong currency substitution and demand for foreign currencies, which could not have been reversed with fixed exchange rates. The reduction of currency substitution required the closing of the gap between the official and the market exchange rates by allowing the official one to float.

The trend of both the nominal and the real effective exchange rate changed after the second half of 1992. The period of depreciation came to an end and the exchange rate started to appreciate considerably. Compared to the highest levels the exchange rate reached in 1992, the appreciation was about 40%, whereas if the base of comparison is the introduction of the new currency, then the appreciation is about 20%.

The reasons for this appreciation are manifold, but contrary to other economies in transition, they are not related to the inflationary performance. The inflation was steadily

41

declining and currently Slovenia has a 1% per month inflation rate which does not create substantial problems for exchange rate management.

The major cause of the nominal and real exchange rate appreciation is related to the changes in the equilibrium conditions on the exchange rate markets. Contrary to the overdemand at the beginning, the market is characterized by oversupply of foreign exchange reserves. The reasons behind this change are the following.

First, as the inflation was reduced and the inflationary expectations were also declining, the money demand was increasing, as both the household and the corporate sectors tried to increase their real balances. However, as the Bank of Slovenia was firmly controlling the domestic credit part of the money supply, the only source of this growth was the swap of foreign currency holdings for tollar.

Second, the supply of foreign currency on the foreign exchange and foreign currency markets was also boosted by the improvements in both current and capital account balances. Slovenia was successful in redirecting its trade from the countries of the former Yugoslavia towards the industrialized economies. Besides, as the country is primarily exporting manufacturing products, it enjoyed improving terms of trade, as the commodity prices were declining while the manufacturing prices were increasing. This led to a substantial increase in exports and resulted in a trade surplus. The impact of trade surplus was augmented by service surplus (mainly due to the revenues from tourism), leading to a significant current account surplus.

The final factor explaining the appreciation of the tollar is related to the capital inflows. They are primarily of a short-term nature associated with speculative capital inflows, reflecting the interest rate differentials on Slovenian and foreign currency denominated returns. As the interest rates are indexed in the country, the real returns are high compared to the international one, which led to the inflow of German and Austrian capital.

These were the factors responsible for the appreciation of the tollar in the last two years. Until now the appreciation did not have a negative impact on the trade balance, as there were competitiveness gains and terms of trade improvements outweighing the impact of the appreciation. On the other hand, the appreciation helped to reduce inflation, the low level of which is explained by the conservative monetary policy, the fiscal surplus and the lack of significant external inflationary pressures.

There are two difficulties in the current situation. First, how the speculative capital inflows will affect the exchange rate developments. These inflows may lead to unfavourably strong appreciation of the tollar, which may no longer be an equilibrium one. The fear from this appreciation is reflected in the measures of the central bank which introduced high reserve requirements on short-term, but partly also on longer-term capital inflows. But it is still not known whether these measures will outweigh the impact of interest differentials which motivate capital to flow in. A related issue is how the competitiveness of the sector of tradables will be affected by this appreciation.

The second problem is the slow convergence of domestic inflation to international levels. This is the primary factor behind the restrictive monetary policy and the high interest rates. As long as inflation differentials remain high, the reduction of speculative capital inflows will be slow.

Conclusions

Having analysed the exchange rate policies pursued by the economies in transition in East-Central Europe, one of the peculiarities of these policies can be found in their variety, in spite of the similarities in the applied macro- and microeconomic policies.

The differences in the pursued exchange rate policies are related to two factors. On the one hand, the initial macroeconomic conditions and the development of the exchange rates before the transition determined the initial choice of the exchange rate regime. In those countries where the exchange rate was overvalued and inflation was high, the policy of steep devaluation with fixing could not be avoided. In those economies, where the official exchange rate was closer to both the market and the equilibrium rates, this pattern of exchange rate adjustment could be avoided.

The second factor explaining the choice of the exchange rate policy is related to the sequencing and the speed of economic reforms. In this respect, the macroeconomic policies and their assumed changes played a crucial role. It made a tremendous difference whether it could be foreseen that the central bank would behave like the Bundesbank and would build up strong credibility and reputation gains (like in the Czech Republic), or its policy would be rather determined by the stance of the fiscal policy and the partial monetary financing of fiscal deficit (like in Hungary or Poland).

Finally, an important factor explaining the choice of the exchange rate regime was the supply of foreign currency reserves. Where there was an oversupply of reserves (or appropriate funds for exchange rate stabilization were provided), the exchange rate regime inclined towards a fixed or pegged one. On the other hand, in economies where the reserves were small at the beginning, the exchange rate policy was more flexible.

Besides these differences, we may also notice some common trends in the exchange rate developments in these economies. First, all of the economies suffered the appreciation of their real effective exchange rates. As a result of this, the exchange rates became closer related to the purchasing power parity exchange rate. The appreciation was – except in Slovenia – the result of high domestic inflation and the use of the exchange rate policy as an anti-inflationary policy tool, and of the inflow of foreign capital. The magnitude of the appreciation was different, depending on the exchange rate regime used by the economies. The Czech Republic and Slovenia suffered the biggest decline in their real effective exchange rate, while the appreciation was relatively small in Hungary and there has been basically no appreciation in Poland since the introduction of the crawling peg regime.

Second, in all economies, there were significant differences in the development of real exchange rate indices if measured with a different price deflator. The most significant differences occurred between the real exchange rate indices when using the CPI and the PPI as deflators. The gap between these two indices is the biggest in Hungary and the smallest in the Czech Republic. The differences in these price indices are related to the differences in the productivity increases in the service and the manufacturing sectors, the different price increases in the sectors of tradables and non-tradables, and to the tax increase associated with the financing of the fiscal deficit. That the difference between the CPI and PPI indices is biggest in Hungary is explained by the fact that, compared to other countries, the productivity increases in manufacturing relative to the service sector and the deficit financing through tax increases are the highest in Hungary.

References

Colombato, E. – Menzinger, J. (1994): Partial Adjustment without Tears: A Tale for the Tollar. In: *The Economies of New Currencies.* Centre for Economic Policy Research, London.

Gotz-Kozierkiewicz, D. – Malecki, W. (1993): Exchange Rate and Foreign Debt in the Monetary Stabilization. Warsaw Institute of Finance, Working Paper.

Hochreiter, E. (1994): The Exchange Rate Policies in Economies in Transition. Mimeo. Wien.

Hrnčíř, M. (1994): The Exchange Rate Policy in the Czech Republic. Mimeo. Prague.

Menzinger, J. (1994): The Experience with the Tollar in Slovenia. In: *The Economies of New Currencies.* Centre for Economic Policy Research, London.

Villanueva, D. (1993): *Options for Monetary and Exchange Rate Arrangement in Transition Economies.* IMF WP/1993/12.

Willett, D. – Al-Marhubi, F. (1994): Currency Policy for Inflation Control in the Formerly Centrally Planned Economies. Claremont Graduate School, Manuscript.

Willett, D. – Al-Marhubi, F. – Dabel, R. (1993): Currency Policies for Eastern Europe and the Commonwealth Countries: An Optimum Currency Area Approach. Mimeo. The Claremont Institute for Economic Policy Studies, USA.

Developments in foreign trade and trade policy in the "Visegrád countries" and Slovenia in 1990–1994

MAGDOLNA SASS

In the process of transition, the importance of foreign trade has changed significantly for all the countries involved. The main reason for this is that trade can serve as one of the few pivots of growth, modernization and structural change in the initial phases of the transition. On the other hand, not only internal factors are involved in the process: these countries also had to cope with external shocks at the beginning of the transformation process, which greatly influenced the internal economy through its effects on foreign trade.

This paper is analysing the foreign trade developments of the "Visegrád countries" (the Czech Republic, Hungary, Poland, Slovakia) and Slovenia. However, the latter country differs from the first four in many respects. First, the size of the Slovenian economy is much smaller (however, in this respect the difference became less significant by the separation of the Czech Republic and Slovakia). Second, its openness is at a much higher level than that of the other countries. The third important element is that because Slovenia is not included in the Visegrád group, there were and are differences in market access, mainly due to the lack of an Association Agreement with the EC (European Community) and until July 1995 with the CEFTA (Central European Free Trade Agreement) countries.

Problems of statistical data

Because of the change and reorganization of statistical systems, the registration problems, the activities of the informal economy, etc., there exist big gaps and discrepancies between the data of the countries in transition and those of the developed ones. Sometimes there are big differences between the data of the national statistics and the mirror statistics. The gap was the biggest in the case of Czechoslovakia, but is less significant in the case of the other countries. However, there are no data available on the regional and the Eastern trade, and no detailed data on the commodity structure, other than those of the national statistics. So the results of the analysis have to be handled with caution.

Trade performance
of the Visegrád countries and Slovenia

In the transitional period of 1990–1994, significant changes characterized the trade developments of all the analysed countries. The most important changes are as follows:

1. In spite of the fall in real GDP, there was only a slight increase in the openness of these countries, measured by the level of exports relative to GDP. (However, the split countries: Slovenia since 1992, and the Czech Republic and Slovakia since 1993, show a higher level of openness, which can mainly be attributed to the fact that a bulk of internal trade processes is now counted as international.) (See Table 1.) The main

Table 1

Changes in the openness of the Visegrád countries and Slovenia
(export/GDP*, %)

	1989	1992	1993		1994
Czechoslovakia	13.2	11.3	Czech Republic:	13.7**	17.6
			Slovakia:	9.0***	19.3
Poland	6.6	7.0	6.6		8.5
Hungary	13.5	18.1	14.9		16.3
Slovenia	...	44.0	38.7		39.9

   * GDP Purchasing Power Parity.
  ** Without trade with Slovakia.
*** Without trade with the Czech Republic.

Source: WIIW, EBRD, national statistics.

reason for this is that the analysed countries could not significantly increase their level of exports, compared to the period before the transition. On the other hand, these similar export levels before and after 1990 differ very much in quality, in the circumstances of competition, etc. Higher openness is mainly due to the fall in GDP. At the same time, imports have increased more significantly for all the countries, mainly in the second phase of the transition – beginning in the second half of 1992 for Hungary and Poland, and in 1993 for the Czech Republic, Slovakia and Slovenia –, while in the starting year of the reform process, and thus in the year of significant import liberalization, there was no surge in imports. The above changes caused deteriorating trade balances in the Visegrád countries and Slovenia. However, the influence of the above factors was different. In the case of the Czech Republic and Slovakia, there was mainly a higher growth of imports, with a later (end-1994, 1995) fall in exports for the Czech Republic; in the case of Hungary, a steep fall in exports, with a much higher growth in imports since 1993; and in the case of Poland, and to a much lesser extent, of Slovenia, both these factors caused the deterioration of the trade balance. (See Table 2.)

2. In the case of all these countries, the geographical structure of trade has changed significantly. After the shock of the demise of the CMEA (Council of Mutual Economic Assistance) and the collapse of the Soviet market (in terms of trade shock, a market loss effect and the removal of the implicit import subsidy on trade with the Soviet Union) (Rodrik 1992), the share of these markets diminished significantly, almost in one step

Table 2
A) Growth rates of export and import
(percentage change in USD values of export and import)

	1989	1990	1991	1992	1993	1994
Czech Republic*						
export	8.5	10.0	39.2	35.2	27.5	8.3
import	−1.5	35.0	29.6	46.2	13.9	17.6
Poland						
export	4.5	43.4	17.5	9.7	−2.9	21.9
import	16.3	17.9	46.9	6.1	17.7	14.5
Hungary						
export	17.1	−1.6	45.9	8.3	−19.3	20.5
import	17.8	1.5	51.2	11.1	12.5	15.8
Slovakia*						
export	8.5	10.1	39.2	35.2	−16.7	23.5
import	−1.5	35.0	29.6	46.2	−12.3	4.2
Slovenia						
export	...	...	−0.6	72.4	−9.0	11.9
import	...	...	−12.6	48.6	5.8	11.5

* Until 1992: Czechoslovak data.

Source: WIIW.

B) Trade balances (billion USD)

	1989	1990	1991	1992	1993	1994
Czech Republic	0.4	1.1	0.4	0.2	0.6	0.0
Poland	−0.1	1.4	−0.8	0.5	−2.3	−2.0
Hungary	0.5	0.3	0.2	0.0	−4.0	−3.8
Slovakia	0.4	−0.8	−0.4	−0.7	−0.9	1.0
Slovenia	...	−0.6	−0.3	0.5	−0.4	−0.4

Source: EDRD (1994), WIIW.

in 1991. The decrease in trade with the smaller former CMEA countries was greater than with the (former) Soviet Union. However, trade among the Visegrád countries has decreased less than trade among the other smaller CMEA countries. This was mainly due to the higher economic development, a more advanced reform process and less significant balance of payment difficulties in the Visegrád countries. The lower decrease in trade with the former Soviet Union can be attributed to the "radial" structure of CMEA trade and to the high energy dependence of the analysed countries on the former Soviet Union.

In the case of Slovenia, similar processes took place by the disruption of economic and foreign trade links with the former Yugoslavia, which resulted primarily in a market loss. In 1992 alone, Slovenian trade with the former Yugoslav republics contracted by almost half, which was mainly responsible for the fall in overall Slovenian exports.

In the case of all the countries, trade with developing countries decreased significantly (an exception is the Czech Republic with her stronger reliance on export to developing countries, which is made possible by the stable foreign trade system), while the share of developed countries, first of all those of the EC, increased. This change took place in different years in each of the analysed countries, due to different economic policy tools and different times of the introduction of reform policies. The change was more pronounced on the export than on the import side. This latter can be attributed to the above-mentioned fact that a certain level of dependence on energy imports from the former Soviet Union has remained for all these countries. (See Table 3.)

Table 3
Geographical structure of foreign trade of the Visegrád countries and Slovenia (%)

| | 1988 | 1991 | 1992 | 1993 | | 1994 | |
				Czech Republic	Slovakia	Czech Republic	Slovakia
Czechoslovakia							
Export							
Total	100.0	100.0	100.0	100.0	100.0	...	...
Developed countries	32.8	52.1	63.7	55.8	30.6	...	...
EC	20.0	40.7	49.4	43.6	24.3	...	...
Developing countries	16.6	14.5	1.7	10.8	10.9	...	...
(former) CMEA	50.6	33.1	24.6	33.4	58.5	...	...
(former) Soviet Union	29.8	19.9	10.9	7.5	8.3	...	...
Import							
Total	100.0	100.0	100.0	100.0	100.0	...	...
Developed countries	37.0	51.5	62.6	60.1	38.6	...	...
EC	21.7	34.3	42.1	42.3	20.9	...	...
Developing countries	13.4	10.6	6.1	5.7	8.1	...	...
(former) CMEA	49.6	37.9	31.3	31.2	61.9	...	...
(former) Soviet Union	27.5	29.8	24.6	14.0	22.9	...	...
Hungary							
Export							
Total	100.0	100.0	100.0	100.0		100.0	
Developed countries	39.5	67.2	71.3	73.0		72.0	
EC	22.1	45.7	49.7	46.5		50.9	
Developing countries	15.9	13.5	9.3	4.1		3.9	
(former) CMEA	44.6	19.3	19.4	22.8		23.1	
(former) Soviet Union	27.6	14.2	13.1	15.3		11.2	
Import							
Total	100.0	100.0	100.0	100.0		100.0	
Developed countries	43.3	66.1	69.7	64.9		70.6	
EC	25.1	41.1	42.7	40.1		45.3	
Developing countries	13.0	11.6	6.7	6.9		4.5	
(former) CMEA	43.7	22.3	23.6	28.2		24.0	
(former) Soviet Union	25.1	16.0	16.9	21.1		15.0	
Poland							
Export							
Total	100.0	100.0	100.0	100.0		100.0	
Developed countries	41.3	73.9	71.9	75.2		75.4	
EC	27.1	55.6	57.9	63.3		62.6	
Developing countries	15.6	9.2	12.8	11.6		10.1	
(former) CMEA	43.1	16.8	15.4	13.2		14.5	
(former) Soviet Union	26.0	10.0	9.5	6.3		...	
Import							
Total	100.0	100.0	100.0	100.0		100.0	
Developed countries	43.2	68.8	72.4	76.3		75.2	
EC	26.7	49.7	53.1	57.3		57.5	
Developing countries	13.7	12.4	11.4	10.3		10.5	
(former) CMEA	43.0	18.8	16.5	13.4		14.3	
(former) Soviet Union	24.8	14.3	12.0	8.2		...	

Table 3 (continued)

	1988	1991	1992	1993	1994
Slovenia*					
Export					
Total	...	...	...	...	100.0
Developed countries	...	...	...	...	72.6
EC	...	...	...	...	59.3
Developing countries	...	...	...	...	6.1
(former) CMEA	...	...	...	...	9.1
(former) Soviet Union	...	...	...	...	4.6
Import					
Total	...	...	...	...	...
Developed countries	...	...	...	...	78.3
EC	...	...	...	...	57.2
Developing countries	...	...	...	...	2.9
(former) CMEA	...	...	...	...	8.5
(former) Soviet Union	...	...	...	...	2.3

* Trade with other partners (first of all former Yugoslavia) add up to 100%.

Source: National statistics.

3. As a result of trade reorientation, the foreign trade turnover of the analysed countries is concentrated on the EC countries, and first of all on Germany, which is the first trading partner for all of them. The concentration is the most pronounced in the case of the Czech Republic (on the basis of national statistics).

In the field of commodity structure, exports to the CMEA countries were and are more concentrated. But together with the fall in the share of (former) CMEA in total exports, the commodity concentration of total exports has declined in the case of all the analysed countries. However, on the import side, this change was less pronounced. Measured by the two-digit SITC (Standardized International Trade Classification) division, the above statements can be proved (Gáspár – Sass 1994). However, on the basis of the calculations of the Hirschman concentration indices, this change seems to be less significant (*Economic Bulletin for Europe* 1993, pp. 127 and 131).

4. The geographical reorientation of trade in the analysed countries is stronger than the reorientation in the commodity structure of their foreign trade. On the basis of calculations in Poland, it was only partly possible to transfer goods from former Eastern trade to trade with the developed countries (Rosati 1993). According to a Hungarian survey, companies could increase their trade with the West mainly by a better utilization of those capacities which were used for export production to the West already before the transition. Concurrently, Hungarian companies decreased the production of those capacities which mainly produced for the Eastern markets (Gáspár – Sass – Szanyi 1993).

The same result can be obtained by calculating similarity indices between the commodity structures of Eastern and Western trade turnover of the analysed countries. These show not increasing, but in some years even declining similarity of the commodity structures in the period of transition compared with the 1980s (Rodrik 1992; *Economic Bulletin for Europe* 1993). (See Table 4.)

Table 4

Change in the commodity structure of foreign trade of the Visegrád countries and Slovenia (%)

Czecho-slovakia export	1987			1992			1993			
							Czech Republic			Slovakia
	total	OECD	CMEA	total	OECD	(former) CMEA	total	OECD	(former) CMEA	
SITC* 0	2.2	8.6	0.7	7.9	7.0	10.1	6.2	5.4	6.4	5.5
1	0.4	0.4	0.5	0.6	0.6	1.1	1.1	0.9	2.3	0.9
2	1.8	7.4	0.8	6.2	7.7	8.0	5.1	2.9	8.6	4.9
3	3.5	10.4	2.2	4.2	4.7	6.5	11.4	1.4	22.8	4.9
4	0.0	0.1	–	0.1	0.0	0.0	0.3	0.5	0.0	0.1
5	6.5	11.8	5.7	9.8	10.5	14.3	12.0	13.8	14.4	12.0
6	16.8	35.0	13.7	35.1	26.9	34.8	15.8	13.5	19.0	38.9
7	56.7	12.1	61.9	9.5	17.7	20.1	35.9	47.1	18.4	19.4
8	11.9	14.2	14.5	22.9	21.7	4.9	11.7	13.8	7.9	13.4
9	0.0	–	–	3.7	0.1	0.2	0.5	0.7	0.2	0.0

Poland export	1988	1993			1994
	total	total	OECD	(former) CMEA	total
SITC* 0	9.4	10.2	10.0	15.5	10.2
1	0.5	1.0	0.2	5.5	1.3
2	6.3	5.5	5.6	4.7	4.7
3	10.2	9.7	9.7	11.8	9.1
4	0.1	0.1	0.1	0.2	0.1
5	8.0	6.8	5.3	14.5	6.8
6	17.4	26.3	25.4	15.8	27.5
7	35.2	20.9	19.8	23.4	19.6
8	8.0	19.4	23.9	8.5	20.5
9	4.9	0.0	0.0	0.0	0.0

Hungary export	1986			1993			1994		
	total	OECD	CMEA	total	OECD	(former) CMEA	total	OECD	(former) CMEA
SITC* 0	16.6	20.9	15.5	16.8	16.6	20.4	16.5	13.7	26.4
1	1.8	0.8	2.8	2.3	0.7	8.0	2.0	6.0	6.4
2	4.0	8.9	1.7	5.7	6.6	4.9	5.2	6.1	3.2
3	4.0	10.1	0.6	4.0	4.4	0.5	4.0	3.5	6.1
4	0.9	1.5	0.4	1.0	0.7	0.6	0.9	0.3	3.0
5	10.9	13.1	8.6	12.1	9.5	15.8	11.2	9.1	15.8
6	10.9	19.8	8.2	16.1	17.0	5.4	16.6	18.2	10.3
7	35.1	11.0	47.8	24.1	19.9	38.7	25.6	26.3	22.5
8	11.9	12.4	13.5	17.8	24.6	5.5	17.9	22.2	6.0
9	3.9	1.5	0.9	0.1	0.0	0.2	0.1	0.0	0.3

Table 4 (continued)

Slovenia export	1985	1993	1994
SITC* 0	7.0	3.9	4.0
1	0.8	0.7	0.7
2	3.0	1.8	1.9
3	0.9	5.1	1.0
4	0.2	0.1	0.1
5	9.7	9.1	10.4
6	27.0	26.1	27.4
7	34.1	27.4	30.3
8	17.3	25.6	24.0
9	0.0	0.2	0.2

Czecho-slovakia import	1987			1992			1993	
	total	OECD	(former) CMEA	total	OECD	(former) CMEA	Czech Republic	Slovakia
SITC* 0	5.3	5.6	2.5	5.7	4.9	7.5	6.2	7.3
1	0.8	0.6	0.9	1.3	1.3	2.6	1.1	1.5
2	7.5	9.4	6.3	6.1	3.6	8.6	5.1	5.2
3	28.8	0.6	43.3	18.8	1.4	17.5	11.3	21.0
4	0.2	0.5	0.1	0.2	0.2	0.3	0.4	0.3
5	6.9	18.1	4.7	9.1	12.4	13.9	12.0	11.3
6	8.6	12.8	7.1	9.3	11.2	18.9	15.9	15.1
7	36.7	44.9	31.0	40.3	53.4	24.0	35.8	29.3
8	5.0	7.5	4.2	9.1	11.5	6.5	11.7	9.0
9	–	–	–	0.1	0.1	0.2	0.4	0.0

Poland import	1988	1993			1994
	total	total	OECD	(former) CMEA	
SITC* 0	11.3	9.7	8.9	5.7	8.6
1	1.2	0.8	0.5	0.4	0.9
2	9.7	4.6	2.9	13.7	5.2
3	14.4	12.5	6.3	42.9	10.5
4	0.7	0.6	0.6	1.0	0.7
5	11.3	13.3	14.6	12.0	14.7
6	13.4	18.5	21.0	12.3	20.3
7	31.6	29.4	34.0	8.6	28.7
8	6.4	10.2	10.7	3.2	9.9
9	0.0	0.4	0.5	0.2	0.0

* SITC 0 = Food and live animals, 1 = Beverages and tobacco, 2 = Crude materials, inedible, except fuels, 3 = Mineral fuels, lubricants and related materials, 4 = Animal and vegetable oils, fats and waxes, 5 = Chemicals and related products, 6 = Manufactured goods classified chiefly by material, 7 = Machinery and transport equipment, 8 = Miscellaneous manufactured articles, 9 = Commodities and transactions not classified elsewhere in SITC.

Table 4 (continued)

Hungary import	1986			1993			1994		
	total	OECD	CMEA	total	OECD	(former) CMEA	total	OECD	(former) CMEA
SITC* 0	5.8	5.0	1.2	5.0	4.6	1.7	5.7	4.7	2.4
1	1.1	1.0	1.3	0.6	0.6	0.2	0.6	0.6	0.2
2	7.0	5.3	6.5	3.1	2.3	5.0	3.7	2.3	8.0
3	20.4	3.4	35.1	13.3	1.7	40.9	11.8	1.9	41.9
4	0.1	0.0	0.0	0.2	0.2	0.1	0.3	0.2	0.3
5	13.7	24.1	7.4	11.9	16.2	5.7	12.7	14.8	8.9
6	16.1	20.9	12.8	18.2	23.6	11.7	19.8	21.4	16.9
7	28.3	31.2	30.3	36.6	36.3	31.0	34.1	40.8	15.8
8	6.2	8.0	3.7	11.1	14.5	3.7	11.3	13.2	5.5
9	1.3	1.1	1.7	–	–	0.0	0.0	0.1	0.1

Slovenia import	1985	1993	1994
SITC* 0	2.7	7.4	7.6
1	0.1	0.7	0.6
2	15.9	5.3	6.5
3	10.7	10.7	7.0
4	0.8	0.4	0.4
5	18.9	11.5	12.3
6	17.4	18.2	19.5
7	30.2	30.3	31.8
8	3.3	12.0	11.0
9	0.0	4.2	3.4

* See note on p. 51.

Source: National statistics.

5. Because the above-described changes are less sector-specific than company-specific, and due to the (still not very pronounced) influence of foreign direct investments, a slow change commenced in the duality of the commodity structure of the analysed countries. It means a commencing change in the former commodity structure, which had been characterized by the dominance of exports of unprocessed goods to the developed countries and exports of manufactured goods to the East. This corresponds with the fact that on the export side, the commodity structure to the CMEA and the developing countries has undergone significant structural changes, while on the import side this change was more pronounced in trade with the developed countries, with a steadily growing share of consumer goods, and to a lesser extent, of other processed products.

6. Parallel with the steep fall of exports to the East, all the analysed countries could dynamically increase their turnover with the West and especially with the EC. However, in the second half of 1992 in Hungary and Poland, and in 1993 and especially from the end of 1994 in the Czech Republic and Slovakia, the dynamics and even the volume of exports to the West have started to diminish. The reasons why this happened later in the Czech Republic and Slovakia can be found in their later start in trade reorientation, in the bigger gap between their real and potential turnover with the West, and in

the macroeconomic policies of the given countries. (In the case of the Czech Republic, subsidies, wage and exchange rate policies; in the case of Slovakia, deeper connections with the East, and ambiguous steps toward market economy are the main factors that influence their trade performance in this respect.)

7. Because of the collapse of former co-operations in the framework of the CMEA and because there was only a slight increase in co-operation with the developed countries, and furthermore, because the inflow or influence of foreign direct investments was lower than expected, inter-industry trade is dominating the trade of the analysed countries, which, however, is on a low level. In the case of Poland, compared to the 1980s, intra-industry trade with the developed countries declined in the analysed period (*Economic Bulletin for Europe* 1993). However, even in the framework of the CMEA, intra-industry trade existed at a lower than possible level, compared to the economic development of the participating countries. In the case of Hungary, because of the greater inflow of foreign direct investments compared to other countries of the region, and because of a higher starting level of intra-industry trade with the EC (Buigues–Ilkovitz 1992, cited by Baldwin 1992), intra-industry trade relations are more developed than in the other countries. Analysis of foreign direct investments into the automotive industry of the Visegrád countries points to the above-mentioned direction. Only joint ventures established in Hungary were able and had a chance to create a network of subcontractors in the domestic economy (Török 1993).

8. On the commodity structure of the foreign trade of the Visegrád countries, only national statistics are available. Because of this, the statements in this section have to be handled with caution. (Comparing Slovenian performance in this respect before and after 1992 is not possible due to the lack of data.) After 1989, in the commodity structure of the total foreign trade, the share of the exports of SITC 7 (machinery and transport equipment), which in the CMEA era dominated the exports of these countries, has decreased significantly. (However, part of this fall in the share of machinery can be attributed to the switch from rouble to dollar prices in the trade between the former CMEA countries.) Moreover, in the case of all the analysed countries, the share of manufactures (SITC 5–8) dominated. In the 1980s, their share exceeded 90% in Czechoslovak exports, they reached almost 80% in Hungarian exports, and almost 70% in Polish exports. (The share of manufactures in exports to other CMEA countries was even higher.) In the case of Czechoslovakia, the fall in the share of manufactured exports was less dramatic than in the case of other Visegrád countries. However, the SITC 7 was replaced by the SITC 6 (manufactured goods) as the most important export commodity group. This phenomenon can be attributed to the delayed restructuring of the Czechoslovak economy and a still relatively high but quickly falling level of exports of manufactured products to the former CMEA (first of all to Russia). In the process of transition, the most important export goods are, on the one hand, mainly unprocessed products: agricultural products for Hungary, coal for Poland and material-intensive manufactured goods for Czechoslovakia (SITC 6). On the other hand, the share of SITC 8 (consumer goods) has increased first in the case of Hungary, then in the exports of Poland and Czechoslovakia as well, due mainly to expanding subcontracting activities.

The change in the commodity structure of imports was less pronounced for all the countries than changes in the export structure. For all of them, the share of fuels (SITC 33) in imports has grown; it is dominating imports from the former CMEA countries (first of all from the Soviet Union). The share of SITC 7 remained the same in total imports in the case of all the Visegrád countries, however, its main country-source is now the OECD (Organization for Economic Co-operation and Development) (and the EC) countries instead of the former CMEA countries. The above-described changes were less pronounced in Czechoslovak imports than in those of the other two countries. However, the Czech Republic and Slovakia "caught up" in this respect later in the period.

9. The similar trade performance (with some time gaps) of the analysed countries is characteristic, in spite of the fact that they had a different heritage, different levels of openness, different weight of trade with the CMEA countries and different burdens of foreign debts from the socialist system, and they followed different paths in their transformation, taking into account the three most important elements of transition: stabilization, institutional reform and modernization. The seemingly different developments in the foreign trade of the Czech Republic and Slovakia in 1993 (higher exports) can be attributed mainly to the effects of the separation. One fifth of the Czech exports went to Slovakia and around two fifths of Slovakian exports went to the Czech Republic. The appearance of these data in international transactions increased the level of exports for both countries. These developments can be found on the import side as well.

The "potential level" of participation of the Visegrád countries and Slovenia in world trade

The "potential level" of trade (openness), the "potential" geographical distribution of trade and the "potential" commodity structures of trade (i.e. based on the comparative advantages) of the Visegrád countries can be assessed by different methods. The level can be estimated on the basis of historical experiences or of trade gravity models. The optimal commodity structure of exports and imports can be assessed on the basis of production factor endowments, and domestic resource costs. (All the methods are burdened with several methodological problems. However, their short description can help in determining the longer term orientation of trade and economic policies of these countries.)

The potential openness ratios, in per cent of exports related to GDP, were calculated for all former CMEA countries by Hamilton and Winters (1992). For the Visegrád countries, the following adjusted potential ratios have been calculated on the basis of the trade gravity model and estimated GNPs: Czechoslovakia 28%; Hungary 31%; Poland 19%. The actual openness of these countries was much below the estimated level in 1985, but these indices are unreliable due to GDP estimation problems and the trade carried out in transferable roubles. However, by 1992, all the analysed countries reached or even surpassed the calculated potential level by official GDP data. (Calculations with Purchasing Power Parity data, however, give different results.) The openness of Czechoslovakia was 28%; that of Hungary 36%; and that of Poland 20% (Fogarassy – Gáspár – Sass 1993). However, in the higher openness, the decline in GDP played a much greater role than the increase in the volume of exports. Only Hungary increased (until 1992) the level of exports compared with 1988. In this respect the other two Visegrád countries experienced a significant decline, Poland almost 10% and Czechoslovakia almost 6% by 1992. However, Hungary followed suit in 1993. The year of 1994 brought an increase for all the countries in this respect.

54

Historical analysis shows that the Visegrád countries always formed part of a bigger economic unit, the centre of which was outside the region, i.e. Austria (in the Austro-Hungarian Monarchy), Germany, the Soviet Union and nowadays Germany again. This central country gave and gives around half of the total foreign trade turnover of the analysed countries. The turnover inside and outside the region was always determined by the above-described relationship. On a geographical basis, there were secondary partners for all the countries, i.e. the Scandinavian countries for Poland, Italy for Hungary and Slovenia, the neighbouring countries for the Czech Republic and Slovakia, and Austria for the latter four countries. Trade relations with the rest of the world remained of marginal importance. On the basis of updating the inter-war (1923) trade matrix for the Visegrád countries – by using information from the evolution of the trade of six compared countries –, Collins and Rodrik (1991) drew the conclusion that the "potential" share of the EC in the foreign trade of these countries could be around 45% for Czechoslovakia, 50% for Poland and 40% for Hungary. The share of Eastern Europe (without the former Soviet Union) is 10%, 9% and 15%, and that of the former Soviet Union 25%, 23% and 33%, respectively.

Another method to estimate the "potential" geographical distribution of foreign trade of these countries is the use of the trade gravity model. On the basis of the estimations of Wang and Winters (1993), using the statistical data of 1985, in the case of Hungary there are only small differences between the results of the historical and the trade gravity analyses. However, in the case of Poland and Czechoslovakia, the share of the EC is on average 5% lower than in the historical model of Collins and Rodrik, and the share of Eastern Europe is on average 5% higher.

If we compare the results of the above analyses with the real geographical patterns of foreign trade of the Visegrád countries, we find that the share of the EC and other developed countries is higher than could be predicted on the basis of the above model, while the share of Eastern Europe (excluding the Soviet Union) is much lower.

In the case of Slovenia, Baldwin (1992) shows that the openness and the geographical distribution of foreign trade are almost equal to those of Austria. This means that Slovenia's further opening, as measured by exports/GDP, cannot be expected. However, on the basis of historical data and geographical proximity, after the end of the civil war in Yugoslavia, the share of the former Yugoslav republics in Slovenian foreign trade could increase with some percentage points.

The "potential" commodity composition of exports and imports of the Visegrád countries was analysed by Hamilton and Winters (1992), Hare and Hughes (1991) and Hughes and Hare (1992). Hamilton and Winters analysed the production factor endowments of the former CMEA countries. Their conclusion is that due to the present level of secondary education, these economies have comparative advantages in the production of medium-tech goods, which require a reasonably trained workforce. However, their prognosis states that these countries have good prospects in catching up with the developed ones, if they continue investing enough into their human and physical capital.

A more formal analysis was conducted by Hare and Hughes. They tried to select industries by positive value added, using world market prices. (This latter poses the problem whether products sold on CMEA markets are identical with those sold on the world market. Because of this and of other methodological problems, the results of this analysis are questioned by many experts.) The authors found that some Hungarian industries, i.e. the footwear, the textile, the chemical and the pharmaceutical industries and the production of electronic equipment, could be competitive on the world market. For Poland the competitive industries were: the production of technical measuring appliances, the food industry and the paper industry; and for Czechoslovakia, the heavy industry.

Hare and Hughes used also a different method to determine the comparative advantages of the former CMEA countries. They tried to list those industries the products of which could be competitive on the world market. In order to do so, they used the concept of domestic resource costs (DRC). However, a full list of methodological problems was enumerated by Drábek (1992) about this concept. (DRC are highly static indicators, shadow pricing does not allow taking into account differences in the quality of products of the Visegrád countries from those sold on the world market, calculations can be made on a too aggregated level, etc.) In spite of this, their calculations have elements of reality, because the most competitive branches in the different analysed countries are differing from each other to a great extent. The five most competitive industries for each Visegrád country are the following: non-ferrous metallurgy, plastic products, machinery, pottery and chinaware, and transport equipment for Czechoslovakia; footwear, leather products, cement, clothing, and structural clay products for Hungary; foodstuffs, printing, tobacco products, instruments and other chemicals for Poland.

The analysis of the recent commodity structures of exports of the Visegrád countries shows a different picture of comparative advantages. The main indicators for analysis of recent trade data were the RCA (Revealed Comparative Advantage) indicator and the trade coverage ratios. Tovias (1991) calculated RCA indices for Hungary on the basis of statistical data on Hungarian foreign trade in the 1980s. He found that Hungarian foreign trade revealed comparative advantages that lay in the so-called "sensitive" sectors, i.e. agricultural products, textile and clothing, steel and branches of chemical industry. On the basis of another analysis (*Economic Bulletin for Europe* 1993), calculated with the trade coverage ratios, the comparative advantages of the Hungarian economy have not changed significantly in the process of transition from those of the 1980s. Comparative advantages can still be found mainly in the processed food and agricultural products, and in low and medium level technical processing in the category of consumer goods. In the case of Poland, revealed comparative advantage can be found in the production of coal, wood and leather in 1992. However, there is a change compared to the 1980s: foodstuff has been dropped from the list of "advantageous" sectors. Czechoslovakian foreign trade revealed that comparative advantages lie in the SITC categories 6 and 8: material intensive manufactures and consumer goods. The SITC 7 category, which was the most "successful" sector in the 1980s, lost its revealed comparative advantages, together with its former CMEA markets. Slovenian comparative advantages lay mainly in SITC 6 and to a lesser extent in some subsectors of SITC 7 product groups.

The examination of the trade data of the Visegrád countries reveals the weakness of the domestic resource costs and the value-added analyses in the case of the former socialist countries. The highly distorted prices and the relative separation of these economies from the world market raise many technical problems which cannot be avoided, and thus the results of the analysis are not backed by the analysis of the real processes. However, the results of Hamilton and Winters (1992), which determine the comparative advantages of the analysed countries in SITC categories 6, and mainly 8, can be proved by the examples of Czechoslovakia and Hungary.

Changes in market access and business cycles on the main markets

Trade reorientation: the new anchor, the EC

As we have seen, trade turnover with the EC has grown dynamically in the case of all the countries. However, the geographical reorientation toward the EC was not followed by a complete reorientation of the commodity structures. The cause of the latter phenomenon can be found partly in the problems of the domestic economy, and partly in changes in the Visegrád countries' access to the EC markets, which determined the foreign trade performance of these countries to some extent in the first stage of the transition, until the end of 1992. In the second stage, with more or less unchanged market access, the deepening recession on these markets had a larger effect.

Although the Association Agreements, concluded between each Visegrád country and the EC, are not inferior in their achievements compared to other similar agreements concluded earlier by the EC, they do not take into account the special circumstances of the transition, under which the Visegrád countries have to be integrated into the world economy. The main reasons why the Association Agreements can be criticized from the point of view of the Visegrád countries are the following: first, the agreements mainly strengthen already existing allowances (however, fixing them for a long period); second, the dynamics of the process of elimination of tariffs does not improve significantly market access in the first difficult stage of transition. Third, the agreements do not open the markets of the EC for the most important export products (the so-called sensitive products: agricultural, chemical, steel, textile and clothing products, on which the exports of the Visegrád countries are concentrated, and which gave about half of their total exports to the EC) (Daviddi 1993); and fourth, the agreements provide both parties with the possibility of using protectionist measures, which were used by the EC in the case of steel and agricultural products (live animals, milk products and sour cherries).

According to an estimation, the complete opening up of markets of the so-called sensitive products for the exporters of the Visegrád countries would cause minimal costs to the EC. Complete unilateral liberalization of these markets would decrease the output of these sectors by only a few percentage points, first of all, in agriculture and in the clothing industry (Messerlin 1992, p. 109 and Rollo – Smith 1993). However, gains in effectiveness and for the consumers due to lower prices would be much higher than the losses in output.

Gains and losses of the Visegrád countries cannot be compared with the above calculations, because there are no estimations about the effects of a further market opening for the Visegrád countries for the exports of the EC (starting only in 1996), due to the asymmetry of tariff reduction. However, the comparison of changes in commodity structures points to the fact that changes in market access, determined by preferential trade agreements, influence the foreign trade performance of the economies in transition only to a limited extent.

On the basis of the above-listed features, the Association Agreements completely fit into the process of the world economy, which started in the 1980s, and which moves in the direction of a so-called "managed" trade (Bhagwati 1992). In this process, new types of trade barriers are emerging, showing signs of growing protectionism. This can be proved by the frequent use of those non-tariff barriers which are not prohibited by the GATT (General Agreement on Tariffs and Trade), first of all anti-dumping. The number of yearly anti-dumping cases grew from 96 to 237 in the period between mid-1992 and mid-1993 (Ostry 1993, p. 10). However, in 1992, an important change took place in this field for the Visegrád countries. The EC has removed these countries from the category of state-trading economies, which in the case of anti-dumping procedures puts them on a basis equal with other countries (Hindley 1993).

In the case of Slovenia, negotiations have started about the conclusion of a similar Association Agreement with the EC and a free trade agreement with EFTA (European Free Trade Association). Until this comes into force, Slovenia has a trade and co-operation agreement with the EC (dated from 1 September 1993). Due to the earlier conclusion of a preferential agreement between the EC and Yugoslavia, the terms of this latter agreement seem to be more favourable in market access than the Association Agreements of the Visegrád countries. According to this agreement, almost all industrial products originating in Slovenia enter the EC duty-free and almost one third of Slovenian agricultural exports enjoys preferential access. Hence, the disadvantageous effects of the civil war and the falling turnover with the former Yugoslavian republics in 1992 were compensated by the effects of the improved market access to the EC, based on the 1993 agreement. (But even the decline of trade with the countries of the former Yugoslavia was gradually coming to a halt in 1993.) Due to the above effects, in spite of the recession on the EC markets, Slovenia could increase her market shares, because the fall in Slovenian exports was smaller than the decrease in the overall imports of the EC (Presern 1994).

For the Visegrád countries there was no significant change in their market access to the EC and thus they were hit stronger by the recession on the EC markets. (However, it is hard to separate the effects of the domestic and the external factors on the foreign trade developments of the countries in transition.) The recession had a twofold effect on EC markets in respect of the exports of the Visegrád countries. First, due to the high income elasticity of imports from these countries, there is a fall in overall import demand and in the level of imports. Second, because of the recession, protectionist lobbies are activated in the EC countries. (These are the most active in the sensitive industries, because they realized that the recession is of a structural character, the consequence of which can be that together with the upturn in business cycles, there will be no significant growth prospects for their branches.)

Regional co-operation and regional trade

Regional co-operation was hit hard at the beginning of the transition by the demise of the CMEA and the economic problems in the countries in transition. In spite of the fact that regional trade between the Visegrád countries has fallen to a lesser extent than the trade between other former CMEA countries, we have already seen that trade in the Visegrád region is much below its potential level.

There were several suggestions – coming mainly from Western sources – about deepening regional co-operation between the Visegrád countries to a certain integrational level. The establishment of a payment union, a regional free trade area and even a deeper level of integration were advised (e.g. van Brabant 1991; Bofinger 1990).

Theories of regional integration identify factors which determine the optimal depth and importance of regional co-operation for the participating countries (Zhang 1993). These are the following: geographical distance between the participating countries; similar level of economic development; complementarity of institutions; similar culture and mentality of people; (political) commitment toward regional integration, and complementarity–competitiveness of foreign trade of the participating countries.

In the case of the Visegrád countries, the above-listed criteria do not back a deep level of regional co-operation. True, they are neighbouring countries, and the level of their economic development – compared to other countries – is similar, and also, they are the best performers in the process of transition among the former socialist countries. However, there are significant differences in their economic policies, and first of all, in the achieved stage of their institutional reform. Even in the mentality, culture and economic thinking of the people there are big differences due to the "strictness" of the socialist system, depending partly on the extent to which the secondary economy existed; and even commitment to regional integration is different. Mainly Poland, but even Hungary represents a pragmatic approach to regional integration, while the Czech Republic hopes to leave the group and be the first to join the EU. Slovakia's approach is rather ambiguous not only to regional integration, but even to reforms. Because of their similar production factor endowments and heritage from the special type of industrialization of the socialist period, the countries of the region are rather competitors than co-operators (Drábek 1992). Moreover, the separation of the Czech Republic and Slovakia introduced significant polarization into the region in every respect listed above.

In the case of the Visegrád region, there were further factors determining the importance of the establishment of a certain form of regional co-operation. First, in order to stop the fall of regional trade, the new agreement about co-operation had to compensate for those trade-diverting and trade-creating effects which were caused by the Association Agreements concluded with the EC, and by the agreements concluded with EFTA. Second, a deeper level of co-operation than the one established with the EC could help the survival of uncompetitive production, because of the lowered level of tariffs and other trade barriers, and thus could hinder the process of restructuring. In these circumstances, the most advantageous form of economic co-operation was the establishment of a free trade zone in the region.

However, the established form of regional co-operation does not completely correspond to the real aims of regional co-operation and poses some technical problems as well. These are the following: first, the agreement covers only a relatively small part of regional trade. On the basis of the data on the turnover in 1992–1993, this part is around half of the bilateral turnovers; but if taking into consideration changes in the commodity structures, this is even less. Second, there still exists the possibility of using non-tariff barriers in regional trade. And the problem is that because of the pressure coming from protectionist lobbies, these are used relatively often. Moreover, because of parallel or similar production structures, the non-tariff barriers, applied normatively, hit mainly the regional partners. (It is interesting that all of the four countries are convinced that the blame has to be put on the other three because of the protectionist tendencies.) Third, the so-called sensitive products are either not included in the timetable of tariff reduction, or they are included in the last stage of it. These products give the majority of the exports of the participating countries in regional trade. Fourth, the conclusion of the CEFTA gave, in principle, the CEFTA exporters in each others' market a similar treatment to that of the EC and EFTA, which could stop the effect of trade diversion. However, the CEFTA compensates for only part of the trade-diverting effects caused by the other two agreements. Moreover, the different commodity structures and schedules of tariff reduction cause temporary, yearly changing trade-diverting and trade-creating effects, which means that exporters and importers of these countries have to face an unstable, almost chaotic environment (Jánszky – Sass 1993).

Because of the above-mentioned trade-diverting effects caused by the EC and the EFTA agreements, extension of the CEFTA to other countries which had concluded similar agreements would be favourable for the countries of the region (Balázs 1993) at least through bilateral agreements concluded by interested CEFTA members, and not by a formal membership. In this respect, the first step was taken by the inclusion of Slovenia into the CEFTA by bilateral agreements, and her membership was announced by the beginning of 1996.

While foreign trade turnover between the CEFTA members has grown significantly following the conclusion of the agreement, we cannot attribute too much influence to the agreement itself in this respect. This can be proved by the little correlation between the sectoral structure of trade liberalization and that of the actual turnover. Reasons for growth in regional trade can be attributed to the economic "recovery" of the countries in question, and to developments in foreign trade between the Visegrád and the developed countries.

Trade relations with the Commonwealth of Independent States

In the case of all the countries, a large fall took place in the foreign trade turnover with the CIS (Commonwealth of Independent States), irrespective of its share in the total foreign trade turnover of the given country. The latter differs very much in the Visegrád countries and Slovenia (the share of the CIS in the foreign trade turnover of Slovenia being less than 4%), because of the different trade orientation of Slovenia before the transition.

For all the countries, Russia is the most important partner among the CIS countries, which is not surprising if we take into account that Russia gives more than 80% of the total foreign trade turnover of the CIS. However, the level of foreign trade of the CIS with the former CMEA remains much below its potential level in the case of all the countries, as we have seen in the analysis of the potential geographical structures of trade. The same is true for trade levels with Russia, as is proved by Rosati (1992), according to whom the potential level of Russian exports to the former CMEA countries in 1991 would have been USD 6.7 billion and that of Russian imports USD 6.5 billion, while in the first eight months of 1993 the actual trade figures were USD 4.2 billion and USD 1.5 billion, respectively. (This latter fact also proves that the geographical reorientation of the Visegrád countries is more pronounced on the export than on the import side.)

Together with the fall in trade turnover, the commodity composition of trade has moved to the direction of turnover in more unprocessed goods (CIS exports consist almost exclusively of raw materials and energy).

The large fall in CIS (and Russian) imports can be attributed to the balance of payments difficulties, to the undervaluation of currencies in real terms, to payment difficulties and to changes in export and import regimes. On the import side, import duties were increased many times, a new import tariff system was introduced on 1 April 1993 and tariff rates were increased in August and October 1993 – all imports are charged with VAT (value-added tax) at the rate of 20% of customs value, plus an excise tax of 10 to 90% on imports of many consumer goods – and the minimum duty-free value was lowered to USD 2000. Other administrative trade barriers (quality requirements, sanitary controls, etc.) are also hindering imports (*Economic Bulletin for Europe* 1993, p. 72).

However, the foreign trade between the two groups of countries can increase in the long run significantly if not only Russia, but also other states build up their foreign trade systems, and if they succeed in stabilizing their economies as well.

A special problem: the consequences of separation in the field of foreign trade (Slovenia and the Czech Republic and Slovakia)

Three out of the five analysed countries have to cope with the problems of separation. This problem is the most pronounced in the case of Slovakia and Slovenia, as they only have a limited experience and institutional framework. The Czech Republic inherited many of the institutions and the majority of the trained staff. In the case of the former two countries, and first of all in Slovakia, this factor hinders effective foreign trade regulation and activities. The second consequence of the separation is that polarization in terms of the level of economic development has grown within the group. This can be found in the changes in the commodity structures of regional trade as well. Thirdly, the level of regional trade has raised due to the fact that former internal flows within Czechoslovakia are now counted as international ones.

Trade and economic policies of the Visegrád countries and developments in the domestic economy as determining factors of foreign trade performances

The foreign trade performances of the Visegrád countries have been affected directly by the trade – export and import – policies, and partly also by the economic policies. In the latter field, stabilization policies and institutional reforms have had their influence on the foreign trade performance of the given country. (The third element of transformation, i.e. restructuring and modernization was not in the forefront of economic policies, and thus its impact cannot be traced in the changes of foreign trade.) Moreover, developments in the real economy, which were sometimes independent of the changes in economic policy, have had their influence as well.

However, it is difficult to separate the influence of external and internal factors on trade developments in the Visegrád countries. In 1990, the dissolution of the CMEA caused significant losses for all the analysed countries, except Slovenia. (For the latter, a similar shock was caused by the Yugoslav separation two years later.) Rodrik (1992) analysed and tried to isolate the external and internal effects. He found that the dissolution of the CMEA and the collapse of the Soviet market made a significant contribution to the fall in real GNPs of the analysed countries. Later, two main factors determined the foreign trade performance of these countries: the effects of devaluations of the exchange rates and the domestic recession. He found that while both were important, domestic recession was the determining factor in 1991 and 1992 from the point of view of foreign trade.

Trade policies

The *liberalization* of foreign trade was introduced in all the countries as part of the stabilization policy, which meant the limitation of direct state control in this field. The main elements of this were the same in all the countries. Economic actors were entitled to carry out foreign trade activities: the extent of the central allocation of foreign exchange was reduced significantly, the scope of licenses diminished and tariffs became the most important tools of trade policy. Tariff levels were different at the beginning of the reform process. Hungary and Slovenia started with higher average tariff levels (16% and 20.5%, respectively), while Poland and Czechoslovakia had lower average rates (8% and 5%, respectively). After modifications, the average tariff levels for all the countries are now fixed around 13–14%. However, there are great differences in the tariff structures, and further modifications were made, first of all, in order to protect the domestic industry and agriculture. Another important tool in this respect is import surcharge, which was introduced by Czechoslovakia in 1991, and survived until the end of 1992. Licensing covers only a limited scope of products in all the countries.

Starting with 1993, the protectionist lobbies became stronger in all the analysed countries, and thus they exercised a considerable pressure on governments to introduce new protective measures. The reason for this may lay in the following factors: first, though at the beginning of the transition, the protectionist lobbies felt defeated, and were weak due to the systemic changes in politics and in economics, at a later point they became active; these protectionst tendencies were strengthened, secondly, by the longer and deeper than expected recession on the domestic markets, and by the higher social costs of the transformation. Third, protectionist groups became active on the developed markets as well, parallel with the deepening recession there. Fourth, the liberalization of foreign trade at the beginning of the reform process was excessive, compared to the similar experiences of the developing countries. This worsened the negotiating positions of the countries in transition in concluding trade agreements with their main partners or international organizations. Fifth, the balance of payments position deteriorated significantly in the case of Poland, Hungary and Slovenia, and later in Slovakia, compared to the beginning of the reform process, which backed the temporary use of protectionist measures. Poland introduced a 6% import tax at the beginning of 1993, and imports were burdened with a further surcharge until December 1994. In Hungary, since October 1993, a quality certificate must be obtained for imported goods, and in March 1995 also an import surcharge was introduced. In March 1994, Slovakia reintroduced an import surcharge of 15% on imported consumer goods. For the same reason, in 1992 and 1993, selective quantitative import restrictions were introduced by all the countries in the fields of agriculture, steel and cement. However, these measures hit mainly each others' exporters because of the similar product structures. Additional protective measures are demanded (and introduced) by major foreign investors in all the countries, e.g. in the car industry.

However, compared to the beginning, the foreign trade regimes at the present stage of the reform process are much more liberal in all the countries. The effect of this was not only a surge in imports, but it also contributed to the export success in the first stage of the transition, e.g. by better access to better quality inputs. This can be partly attributed to the fact that there is a growing number of economic actors in foreign trade, which thus became less concentrated in this respect. However, because of the applied privatization techniques in Poland and Czechoslovakia (and now in the Czech Republic and Slovakia), concentration of foreign trade here decreased much less than in the case of the other two countries.

Partly due to budget problems, partly to the reluctance from direct state intervention, and partly also to the surprisingly successful export performance, none of the analysed countries implemented a kind of *export promotion* policy package. Poland was the first to implement a programme of this kind, but only in 1993. Exporters are exempted from excess wage tax, company tax is reduced in the case of investments, export credit and export guarantee agencies were established, and the Export Promotion Fund started to work at the Ministry of Foreign Trade. In the Czech Republic, except for measures of minor importance, similar institutions were established at the end of 1993. However, the Czech policy-makers do not contemplate the implementation of an export promotion package similar to the Polish one. In Slovakia export promotion is in the same state as in the Czech Republic.

Economic policies

In the first phase of the transition when priority is given to the internal stabilization of the economy, domestic demand is depressed by restrictive monetary, fiscal and income policies. Investments and output decreased significantly in all the countries, which caused a fall, first of all, in demand for investment goods and industrial inputs. However, as a result of institutional changes in foreign trade, which characterized all these countries, and the consequent liberalization and decentralization of foreign trade activities, the opening up of these economies to the world economy, the long-depressed demand – in spite of the fall in aggregate demand – for imported consumer goods had increased. In order to counteract the above-described process of acceleration of imports of consumer goods, Poland and the former Czechoslovakia introduced special taxes on trade. Poland, after the modification of the tariff system in 1989 with higher tariffs on consumer goods, suspended the collection of tariffs on raw materials and investment goods for some months in 1990. That was followed by the introduction of higher tariff rates in 1991, with higher tariffs on sensitive products (Rosati 1994). Hungarian economic policy lacked these types of measures. As it was mentioned, quality control, as an administrative trade barrier, was introduced on imported goods only in 1993. However, in spite of the above-described factors, the foreign trade data indicate that imports started to increase in all the analysed countries.

On the other hand, the fall in domestic demand caused an increase of exports in these countries. In the former Czechoslovakia, for example, in 1991 the fall in aggregate demand was caused by a 60% contraction of the domestic consumer market and by a 20% contraction of the domestic market for investment goods. Thus, the companies, the main aim of which was to survive, and which could count on help from the state, tended to sell their products on Western markets, sometimes much below the production costs.

Actually, lower prices than the world market ones always characterized Eastern exports to the West. This phenomenon was only strengthened by the above-described problem. The extent of "undervaluation" can be proved by the estimations of the Instytut Koniunktur i Cen in Warsaw, cited by Misala (1994), according to which Poland could have obtained USD 14.7 billion instead of 9.5 billion for the goods exported in 1992, if the prices obtained were equal to the respective prices on the world market.

However, because of the lack of investments, new export capacities were not established in the process of transition, some exporting firms even went bankrupt, e.g. in Hungary, while some others were closed down, e.g. in the field of the Czech and Slovak military industry. The ineffective exports could not be financed forever, and this, together with the lack of export capacities, caused a deceleration or even a fall in exports in all the countries in the second phase of the transition.

At the same time, exchange rates, which played the role of a nominal anchor in the stabilization policies, were devalued significantly at the beginning of the reform process in Poland and Czechoslovakia. Thus exports (even inefficient exports) were promoted and imports hindered. But in the second phase of the reform process, because of the differences in the inflation rates, the exchange rates appreciated significantly in the case of all the countries. According to IMF (International Monetary Fund) International Financial Statistics, the domestic currencies were overvalued in real terms in almost the whole of the analysed period (1989–1993) in the case of Hungary and Poland, and the same is true for the Czechoslovak currency after 1992 and for the currencies of the split countries since 1993. Other estimates state an overvalued position for the Hungarian currency since the middle of 1992, and an undervalued one for the Polish zloty until 1995 and for the Czech and Slovakian currency for the whole period. In the case of Slovenia, which used a floating exchange rate regime, the real appreciation of the currency was not so pronounced. Even the increased demand for imports and thus for foreign exchange caused a real depreciation of the currency in 1993 by 8%, on the basis of estimations (Vidovic 1994).

As part of the stabilization policies, *fiscal policies* became restrictive in all the analysed countries at the beginning of the reform process. A restructuring of revenues (introduction of VAT, personal income tax) and expenditures (reducing subsidies and social expenditures), parallel to the deteriorating trade balance and increasing new types of social costs, maintained the heavy tax burden on companies (and individuals). Considering the direct effects on trade policy, customs duties form a significant part of revenues in the transitional countries, compared to developed countries. For example, in the case of Japan, customs duties give less than 1% of total revenues of the budget, while this proportion in the case of Hungary is around 20%. In the Czech Republic, the role of customs duties is smaller than in the other countries of the region. For example, it gave only around 3% of the total revenues of the budget in 1993 (*The Czech Republic...* 1993, p. 21).

While the comparative advantages of the analysed countries lay mainly in their relatively skilled, but relatively cheap labour, taxes on the use of this resource can have significant distorting effects on their export performance. The analysed countries form two groups in this respect. While Poland, the Czech Republic and Slovakia had an excess wage tax in the majority of the period, in Hungary and Slovenia *wage controls* were suspended in 1992. In Poland, the excess wage tax was introduced in 1986, and is charged on wage increases exceeding the predetermined growth rates, linked to the current inflation rate (Rosati 1994, p. 49). A similar type of wage regulation was introduced in the former Czechoslovakia at the beginning of the reform process, where enterprises with more than 25 employees had to pay taxes on the growth of wages exceeding an agreed level. Joint ventures and private companies were exempt from this regulation. This type of tax was several times suspended and reintroduced in the split countries. While this system helps to keep real wages low, on the other hand, it helps to maintain over-employment, and keeps the labour market rigid – as can be seen from lower unemployment data of the Czech Republic –, and thus hinders industrial restructuring. Moreover, because of the effect on the relative prices of labour and capital, wage controls favour labour intensive industries.

In contrast to the above systems, in Hungary wage controls were at first minimized in 1992 and then completely abolished in 1993. However, the case of Slovenia is not so "clear" in this respect. After the expiry of the law on wage controls in 1992, (unsuccessful) collective wage agreements were concluded, which tried to freeze wages until the end of 1993. In 1994 another attempt was made to stop further increases in real wages and incomes. These policy measures – sometimes contrary to their objectives – caused substantial real wage increases in both countries, the consequence of which was that subcontracting activities, which in the case of Hungary gave about 70% of the export growth in 1992, started to move to countries with lower wages. Surprisingly, after 1993 subcontracting activities started to grow again in Hungary, in spite of the higher real wages compared to the other countries. The other consequence of the rise in real wages was higher consumption in Slovenia, which boosted imports of consumer goods and thus contributed to the deteriorating trade balance. Because of this, the Slovenian government reintroduced a new system of wage control in 1993, which caused a moderate decline in real wages later that year, and a decreased demand for imported consumer goods, and thus helped to maintain the foreign trade balance.

A trade pattern can be influenced by taxes on the use of capital as well. In Poland, a so-called *dividend tax* has to be paid by all state-owned enterprises on the value of their fixed assets, irrespective of their economic performance (Rosati 1994). The dividend tax penalizes the capital intensive sectors – especially those with high tech equipment – and has the same effect on exports as wage controls have.

As part of the price liberalization, the share of *subsidies* was reduced in all the Visegrád countries and Slovenia at the beginning of the reform process. The further decrease of subsidies has been backed by the deteriorating budget balance, except for Czechoslovakia. While the level of subsidies is similar in all the countries, their structure is different and, together with the tax structure, results in different energy prices. Dietz (1993) analysed prices of energy in Hungary, Poland and Czechoslovakia. He found that in 1991 Hungarian users of fuels paid world market prices, while Polish and Czechoslovakian consumers paid lower prices. The difference is much bigger in the case of coal and electricity. Lower energy prices can favour more energy intensive production and exports, which is the case according to Rosati's analysis (1992). Analysing both the private and the public sectors, he found that the trade structures show a distinct bias in favour of the more energy intensive exports to the EC.

Budget problems have an indirect negative effect on foreign trade performance in Hungary and Poland, where the method of financing a growing budget deficit by government bonds has a crowding-out effect on credit to companies. Commercial banks want to make up for the difference in the costs of funding that they incur by having to compete with low-risk, high-rate government bonds, by offering – partly due to the high compulsory reserve ratios – expensive credits to companies. Thus interest rates are high and real deposit rates – because of the higher inflation rates – have become negative.

Furthermore, the market economy links between companies and banks are not working. In the case of the former Czechoslovakia, credit is offered to companies at a lower rate, but the real costs of credit are negative for the companies, and thus the banking system is financing the ineffective production of companies as well, which increases the bad debts of the banking system and causes queueing for the companies.

Conclusions

It is difficult to summarize and to find general trends in the foreign trade performances and the foreign trade policies of the Visegrád countries and Slovenia. This can be explained by the shortness of the analysed period and by the lack of reliable statistical data. However, the following findings have to be emphasized. In all the countries – together with a reorientation of foreign trade towards the developed countries – there was a (slight) move towards a foreign trade structure which is based on comparative advantages.

On the other hand, while outside factors influenced the foreign trade performance of the analysed countries significantly, first of all in the first period of transition, the determining factor in this respect is their economic policy. From this aspect, not only some elements of trade policy or policy measures directly influencing foreign trade have to be taken into account, but literally the whole of economic policy. And this is what can explain the similarities and differences in the foreign trade performances of the analysed countries.

References

Balázs, P. (1993): A szabadkereskedelem újjászületése Európában (The revival of free trade in Europe). *Közgazdasági Szemle,* No. 1.

Baldwin, R.E. (1992): *An Eastern Enlargement of EFTA...* Graduate Institute for International Studies, Geneva and CEPR.

Bhagwati, J. (1992): *The World Trading System at Risk.* Harvester-Wheatsheaf.

Bofinger, P. (1990): *A Multilateral Payments Union for Eastern Europe?* CEPR Discussion Paper No. 458, London.

Brabant, J. M. van (1991): *On Reforming the Trade and Payments Regimes in the CMEA.* Jahrbuch der Wirtschaft Osteuropas, No. 2.

Collins, S. M. – Rodrik, D. (1991): *Eastern Europe and the Soviet Union in the World Economy.* Institute for International Economics, Washington.

Daviddi, R. (1993): Commercio e aiuti nelle relazioni tra la Cee e l'Europa dell'Est. *Politica Internazionale,* No. 1, January–March 1993.

Dietz, R. (1993): *Energy Markets in Transition. The Case of End User Price Changes in Czechoslovakia, Hungary and Poland.* WIIW Forschungsberichte, No. 194, March.

Drábek, Z. (1984): A Comparison of Technology in Centrally-planned and Market-type Economies. *European Economic Review,* vol. 25, pp. 293–318.

Drábek, Z. (1992): Payments Union, Costs of Production and Trade Complementarity in Central and Eastern Europe. In: *External Economic Relations of the Central and East European Countries.* Colloquium 1992. Brussels, NATO.

Economic Bulletin for Europe (1993): UN Economic Commission for Europe. Geneva, Switzerland, No. 44.

Fogarassy, G. – Gáspár, P. – Sass, M. (1993): A visegrádi országok gazdasági fejlettségének, a piacgazdasági átalakulásba való előrehaladottságának összehasonlítása (Comparison of the economic developments and the progress in market-economic transformation of the Visegrád countries). Institute for World Economics, Hungarian Academy of Sciences.

Gáspár, P. – Sass, M. (1994): Inserting Hungary into the International Division of Labour. Paper prepared in the framework of the ACE-project "Inserting Central Europe into the International Division of Labour". Budapest.

Gáspár, P. – Sass, M. – Szanyi, M. (1993): The Export Performance of Hungarian Companies in the Process of Transition. Manuscript. Institute for World Economics, Hungarian Academy of Sciences, Budapest.

Hamilton, C. B. – Winters, L. A. (1992): Opening up International Trade with Eastern Europe. *Economic Policy*, No. 2.

Hare, P. – Hughes, G. (1991): *Competitiveness and Industrial Restructuring in Czechoslovakia, Hungary and Poland*. CEPR Discussion Papers.

Hindley, B. (1993): *Helping Transition through Trade? EC and US Policy towards Exports from Eastern and Central Europe*. EBRD Working Paper No. 4, March.

Hughes, G. – Hare, P. (1992): *Competitiveness and Industrial Restructuring in Czechoslovakia, Hungary and Poland*. CEPR Discussion Paper Series No. 543, London.

Inotai, A. – Sass, M. (1994): *Economic Integration of the Visegrád Countries: Facts and Scenarios*. Institute for World Economics, Hungarian Academy of Sciences, Working Papers No. 34.

Jánszky, Á. – Sass, M. (1993): *A visegrádi országok gazdaságpolitikája és külkapcsolatai, a preferenciális szerződésekből eredő versenyelőnyök és hátrányok* (The economic policy and foreign relations of the Visegrád countries, the advantages and disadvantages caused by their preferential trade agreements). OMIKK, Budapest.

Messerlin, P. A. (1992): Az EK és a kelet-közép-európai országok társulási szerződései (The Association Agreements of EC and the East-Central European Countries). *Európa Fórum*, No. 2, September.

Misala, J. (1994): Foreign Trade Development Tendencies of Poland in 1990–1993. Manuscript.

Ostry, S. (1993): *The Threat of Managed Trade to Transforming Economies*. EBRD Working Paper No. 3, March.

Presern, N. (1994): *Economic Perspectives for Slovenia*. SKEP, Chamber of Economy of Slovenia.

Rodrik, D. (1992): Foreign Trade in Eastern Europe's Transition: Early Results. NBER, Manuscript.

Rollo, J. – Smith, A. (1993): The Political Economy of Eastern European Trade with the European Community. Why so Sensitive? *Economic Policy*, April, No. 16, pp. 140–183.

Rosati, D. K. (1992): *After the CMEA Collapse: Is the Central European Payments Union Really Necessary?* Foreign Trade Research Institute, Warsaw, Discussion Papers No. 18.

Rosati, D. K. (1993): Poland: Glass Half Empty. In: Portes, R. (ed.): *Economic Transformation in Central Europe: A Progress Report*. European Community, pp. 211–274.

Rosati, D. K. (1994). *Changes in the Structure of Manufactured Trade Between Poland and the European Community*. Foreign Trade Research Institute, Warsaw. Discussion Papers No. 49.

The Czech Republic in the International Economy (1993). Centre for Foreign Economic Relations. Prague, December.

Török, Á. (1993): Privatizáció, strukturális alkalmazkodás, kivitel (Privatization, structural adjustment, export). *Külgazdaság*, pp. 17–30.

Tovias, N. (1991): EC–Eastern Europe: A Case-Study for Hungary. *Journal of Common Market Studies*, No. 3.

Vidovic, H. (1994): *Die Wirtschaft Sloweniens und Kroatiens*. WIIW Forschungsberichte No. 79.

Wang, Z. K. – Winters, L. A. (1993): *EC Imports from Eastern Europe: Iron and Steel*. EBRD Working Paper No. 9.

Zhang, Z. (1993): Revival of Regional Economic Integration – Challenge for the Asian Pacific Region. EUI Working Paper EPU, No. 93/1.

Employment and unemployment in the "Visegrád countries" and Slovenia

KLÁRA FÓTI

Introduction

The number of people out of work has been increasing in this region where in most countries, with the exception of the former Yugoslavia, open unemployment had not existed for decades. (And if there was any, it was not admitted.) At the same time a virtually unknown phenomenon in the developed countries characterized the economies of the region, namely: the co-existence of labour shortage and labour hoarding (i.e. overemployment). This has contributed with serious imbalances to the recent unprecedented rapid rise of unemployment in these countries.

Although it is doubtful whether the reasons for the shortage, i.e. the soft budget constraints as well as an underdeveloped and distorted industrial structure, have all been fully eliminated, in most cases unemployment has already risen to a level above that of the OECD (Organization for Economic Cooperation and Development) countries (the number of job-seekers having reached about 4 million people in the five countries under consideration). Basically this is a consequence of the effects of economic transformation. In four out of the five countries, the collapse of the CMEA (Council of Mutual Economic Assistance) also contributed to rising unemployment, whereas in the case of Slovenia, the disruption of trade relations with the other republics of the former Yugoslavia had similar effects.

Even prior to the transition, the labour market did exist in these countries insofar as jobs were not allocated by planners and workers were able to choose their work and location (in East-Central Europe the practice of job assignment was common only in the 1950s and later it was abolished, unlike in China where it existed until recently). Undeniably, the labour market was dissimilar to the Western one in an important respect. With the exception of Slovenia,[1] wage setting was highly centralized and bureaucratic, and was done by state authorities instead of collective bargaining which has been established only recently. This obviously led to rigidity in the labour market, which was exacerbated by rigid employment forms (dominance of full-time jobs) deriving mainly from the overwhelming dominance of the state sector.

Despite the initially similar features of labour market structures, one should be cautious in making an exclusively data-based comparison between these countries, partly because unemployment statistics are still in an early phase and partly because of the expansion of the hidden economy. Although in all the analysed countries labour force surveys, using internationally accepted common definitions and standards, are carried out on a regular basis, they were introduced only around 1992 in most cases. As far as registration figures are concerned, the frequent changes and differences in eligibility

---

[1] As a result of the system of self-management, wage setting was decentralized and workers had much say in it.

conditions make it difficult to apply a direct comparison of these data across countries, not to mention the growing problem of long-term unemployment, which is difficult to be measured with registration data (especially in the case of people who dropped out of any kind of compensation because their entitlement period expired and thus they are no longer registered). In addition, the hidden economy seems to be gaining ground to a large (and certainly diverse) extent in almost all Central and Eastern European countries, adding to the problems of measuring the real size of unemployment. Therefore, an exclusively data-based comparison can be misleading. That is the reason why this paper prefers to highlight some *macro- and microeconomic factors which explain the diversities between the countries under consideration.* At the same time, it makes an attempt to identify some specific common features of the transition, which distinguish the Central and Eastern European labour markets from those in the established market economies.

The impacts of the adjustment process on the labour market are ambiguous and currently the negative effects seem to dominate – not least due to rising unemployment. One of the most important reasons for the drastic fall in employment lies in a major decrease in output in the wake of contracted foreign and domestic demand,[2] which also relates to the difficulties of the transformation process e.g. in agriculture. Abolishing labour hoarding is also sometimes mentioned as a reason for declining employment. No doubt, this is also part of the adjustment process, but empirical evidence has not supported this view in all cases.

With the exception of Slovenia, in all the former Central and Eastern European socialist states, including those where some elements of a market economy had already existed, unemployment was virtually an unknown phenomenon during the communist period (although its seasonal and frictional forms were occasionally present, their existence was never admitted). Now mass unemployment may potentially be a major source of social tension undermining the whole transformation process. That is why labour market policy is of crucial importance, though it has major challenges to face. These challenges are deriving not only from the legacy of the communist regime, but also from the present state of these economies. With the number of people out of work increasing and long-term unemployment expanding, the growing needs are constantly confronted with the very limited financial resources. Although the problem is familiar in the OECD countries too, in Central and Eastern Europe the conflict is emerging on a much larger scale. So apart from improving the efficiency of labour market policy measures by adapting them to the specific requirements of transition, there is also an urgent need to explore those macroeconomic conditions, which could contribute to easing the labour market imbalances.

Economic activity and employment

As is well known, the level of economic activity is higher in these countries than in the developed ones, due to the much greater involvement of women in the labour force.[3] It is not surprising therefore that the recession and the transition process have led to

---

[2] Contraction of foreign demand is associated not only with the collapse of the CMEA, but also with the current recession and the subsequent protectionist tendencies prevailing in the world economy, including the European Union as the most important trading partner of these countries.

[3] This is the consequence of the so-called extensive industrialization of the 1950s.

lower participation, and the decrease was greater than in the developed countries during economic downturns. Lower activity level can be clearly seen from Table 1. Between 1989 and 1993, activity rates dropped by 0.6–8 percentage points in the respective countries.

Table 1
Activity rates in some East-Central European countries (1989–1993)
(economically active population as a percentage of working-age population)

Year	Czech Republic	Hungary	Poland	Slovakia	Slovenia
1989 total	93.0	85.3	75.6	86.3	
male	95.5	84.7	82.6	91.6	
female	90.3	85.8	68.6	80.4	
1990 total	89.3	85.3	75.0	83.3	
male	91.4	84.8	81.5	87.9	
female	86.9	85.7	68.4	78.4	
1991 total	87.8	84.0	75.3	82.5	
male	92.4	84.3	80.5	89.3	
female	82.4	83.6	70.1	75.3	
1992 total	85.0	81.7	75.0	80.8*	80.1**
male	91.6	80.8	81.3	87.7	81.9**
female	77.7	82.8	68.9	73.4	78.2**
1993 1st quarter					
male	86.5	78.8	86.6		
female	83.6	71.2	69.9		
1993 2nd quarter					
male	86.3	78.7	86.4		
female	82.7	71.1	69.9		

Sources: For the Czech Republic, Slovakia and Poland: *Employment Observatory;* for Hungary until 1992: *Labour Force Accounts,* Central Statistical Office; for Slovenia: *Employment Barometer, Centre for Welfare Studies,* 1993.

  * Estimate.
** Own calculations, based on *Labour Force Surveys.*

Notes:
1. In the Czech Republic before 1993 data on the active population exclude women on unpaid maternity leave, whereas in the case of Hungary, women on paid maternity leave are included.
2. Data for 1993 come from *Labour Force Surveys* (LFS) in all cases.
3. Figures for Poland exclude civilians in armed forces.
4. In the case of Hungary, until 1993 figures refer to January 1 each year.

It is remarkable that the activity rate declined by the highest value (by 8%) in the Czech Republic, where the unemployment rate is the lowest. A fall in the activity rate is the only answer to the question "where have all the jobless gone" without becoming actually unemployed (i.e. how could unemployment drop amidst a 4.2% decrease in employment[4]).

Throughout Central and Eastern Europe, the fall in the activity rate can be traced back basically to three sources:

(1) Early retirement schemes rapidly gaining ground, especially in Slovenia, Hungary, the Czech Republic and Poland. In Poland, an estimated one million persons took advan-

---

[4] See Janácek (1993) quoted by Koltay (1994).

tage of this scheme;[5] whereas in Hungary, about 100,000 people retired due to labour market reasons; in the case of the Czech Republic, 70,000 persons were affected between 1990 and 1992.

(2) Increased intake to the institutions of higher education (universities and colleges) to avoid high youth unemployment (this was the case, for example, in Hungary).

(3) Leaving the labour force, women sometimes opted to stay at home (however, as is apparent from Table 1, this phenomenon was sporadic and was more characteristic in the former Czechoslovakia than in Hungary or Poland).

All the three sources can be regarded basically as a response to the rise in unemployment, so there is no doubt that they are closely associated with the growing labour market imbalances.

Employment has dropped in all countries since 1989, but it generally fell in industry to a lesser extent than the decline in output. Perhaps Slovenia could be regarded as an exception in this respect. According to Slovenian experts (Drobnic 1993; Kajzer 1994), employment was very responsive to economic activity. Mencinger (quoted by Drobnic 1993) estimated that a 1% fall in output in the business sector led to a 0.68 decline in employment over the period 1991–1992. However, this figure may not be comparable to data in other former socialist countries, because the calculation is likely to be different.

As regards Hungary, Boeri and Keese (1992) estimated a low (though slightly increasing) figure for an earlier period: between 1980 and 1985, a 1% output decline led to a 0.03 fall in employment, whereas this figure stood at a level of 0.05 in the period 1986–1991.

The low response of employment to the fall in output may be at least partly attributed to the fact that in almost all countries of the region (with the exception of Bulgaria, which we are not considering), legislation limited massive dismissals. In the case of group dismissals, companies are obliged to pay heavy severance payments. Since most of the state-owned or recently privatized companies are in a weak financial situation, they could hardly afford to meet these obligations. Therefore, they had to "invent" other methods: so did short-time working arrangements or forced (unpaid) leave periods, or the reduction of the number of shifts become the preferred methods of adjusting employment to output decline.[6] (These methods obviously imply decreasing capacity utilization, as suggested by empirical evidence.)

The arguments saying that the provisions limiting mass dismissals make the labour market more rigid are very convincing, especially if we regard severance payments, which are usually generous even compared to the OECD countries.[7] However, bearing in mind those specific circumstances[8] within which mass unemployment emerged in these countries, this kind of legislation seems to be justifiable, at least for the time

[5] See Karpinska-Mizielinska – Smuga (1993), p. 7.

[6] In the case of all those countries where data on hours worked in industry are available, the figures prove the presence of these methods: in most cases output per hour declined less than output per person (again the exception being the Czech Republic). See Boeri (1993), p. 8.

[7] That is the case, for example, in Hungary.

[8] Unemployment was rising at an unprecedented rate in these countries where open unemployment was practically unheard of until the political changes, and therefore the appropriate labour market institutions as well as an appropriate safety net were virtually lacking and employment forms were much more rigid than those in the developed countries (e.g. part-time employment was very rare).

72

being, as they help prevent major social tensions, which could undermine the transformation process.

There were high expectations concerning the job-creating capacity of the newly emerging private sector to counterbalance the losses in employment in the state sector. However, the majority of these expectations proved to be an illusion.

Although it is true that due to the private sector's expansion, hirings exceeded dismissals in this sector in most countries, but in none of the cases could they counterbalance the dismissals from the state sector. Moreover, in Poland, where (like in Slovenia) the private sector was relatively large prior to the transition, the opposite process started in 1992 (dismissals exceeded hirings).[9] This fact is not very encouraging for the future perspectives of other countries.

In most of the countries under consideration, the new small and medium-sized companies (especially the domestic ones) have to face serious macroeconomic and other constraints, such as: lack of capital, high interest rates, infrastructural shortcomings, high taxation, lack of experience, etc. The other reason explaining the private sector's low absorbing capacity lies in its pattern of labour demand, which greatly differs from the supply pattern of those released from the state sector.

For example, a Hungarian survey conducted in 1992 showed that the private sector needed more skilled labour than the state sector: the share of unskilled and semi-skilled workers in the private sector is half of that in the state sector (in the case of the unskilled workers, the gap is even wider, their share in the state sector being 12% versus 4% in the private sector).[10]

The same applies to the majority of the newly established companies with foreign ownership or joint ventures. In addition, high non-wage costs such as: extremely high social security contributions especially in Poland and Hungary; employers' contributions to labour market policy measures; high severance payments, etc., make them cautious in new hirings. The Hungarian domestic private sector's response to high labour costs seems to be different. This sector is very adversely affected by the mentioned macroeconomic constraints, especially by the lack of capital and the high interest rates.[11] In addition, in Hungary in order to attract foreign capital, foreign companies have so far enjoyed a more preferential treatment than domestic entrepreneurs. So, unsurprisingly, under-reporting of wages in the domestic private sector seems to be a widely applied "survival strategy" (it is difficult to prove such cases, since both the employers and employees are interested in minimizing these – otherwise serious – burdens on payroll and on income, respectively[12]). A similar phenomenon can be observed in Slovenia: a large part of private sector employment has been done on a contractual basis, supposedly because in this case payments of appropriate social benefits could be avoided. This had led to changes in the tax system in 1994, which penalize such practices.[13]

---

[9] Boeri (1993).

[10] See: Bukodi – Harcsa – Reisz (1994).

[11] Foreigners are in a more favourable position, since they can borrow on international financial markets, so they can offset the highly unfavourable internal macroeconomic conditions.

[12] There are several cases in Hungary, known by the author, in which private entrepreneurs follow this practice. It must be widespread, especially in the case of young male employees, since besides unemployment compensation and sick leave, only some of the maternity provisions depend on income. However, in the case of older employees, being close to retirement age, this is not a viable option due to the income-related pension system.

[13] I am grateful to Sonja Drobnic for this information.

The third reason explaining the private sector's small employment-generating capacity lies in low labour mobility, which also relates to regional dispersion in unemployment. As a study on Hungarian regional unemployment has pointed out, entrepreneurial capacity is usually low in the traditional centres of "socialist" industry, characterized now by mass release of workers from the state sector.[14]

The limited role of the private sector in employment is apparent from the fact that even during the period of some recovery, employment does not grow. Poland is an illustrative case in this respect. Here industrial production increased by 4.2% but employment continued to drop by 7.8% in 1992 (previously employment fell to a lesser extent than the industrial output; in 1990 the respective figures were –5.9% as opposed to –24.2%, whereas in 1991 the output fell by 11.9% and employment by 8.6%)[15] (see Table 2). Indisputably, there seem to be serious difficulties in assessing the role of the private sector in employment, since its statistical coverage is still problematic.

Table 2
Changes in output and employment from 1990 to 1992 (%)

Country	1990		1991		1992	
	Output	Employment	Output	Employment	Output	Employment
Czech Republic	–3.8	–6.4	–25.6	–15.3	–11.1	–5.6
Slovakia	–4.1	–2.0	–35.4	–14.9	–14.7	–8.1
Poland	–24.2	–5.9	–11.9	–8.6	24.2	–7.8
Hungary	–9.1	–10.6	–23.9	–3.9	–2.0	–22.2
Slovenia**	–10.5	–4.5*	–12.5	–8.6*	–13.5	–7.0

Sources: OECD, Short-Term Economic Indicators, OECD, CCET Labour market database (Boeri 1993) and Annual Report 1992, Bank of Slovenia (Kajzer 1994).

* Figures cover the so-called social sector only.
** Private companies employing three or more persons are also included.

In the case of Hungary, for example, the estimates range between 17 and 33% (Bukodi – Harcsa – Reisz 1994; Bossányi 1993); data vary according to sources also in Poland: some sources say that in 1992 employment in the private sector exceeded that in the state sector, engaging 56.6% of the employees (Central Statistical Office in Warsaw[16]), whereas according to others, its employment share is 44.4%.[17] As regards Slovenia, about 18% of the active population is engaged in the private sector (self-employed and employees; according to the Employment Office of Slovenia, Ljubljana[18]).

The sectoral pattern of employment also changed considerably in most cases. Although the structure seemingly shifted towards the service sector in all the countries

[14] See Fazekas (1993).

[15] Karpinska-Mizielinska and Smuga explain this with a delay effect. It certainly seems to be true, especially if we take into account the legislation limiting group dismissals: for example, in 1990, the share of those among the unemployed who were involved in group dismissals accounted for only 16%, whereas the figure increased to 24% by December 1992 (Boeri et al. 1993, p. 20). However, it remains to be seen whether the delay effect will be at work in the long run as well.

[16] See Karpinska-Mizielinska – Smuga (1993).

[17] See *Employment Observatory* (1992, 1993) (quoted by Koltay 1994).

[18] See Drobnic (1994).

74

under consideration, taking a closer look at it reveals that this phenomenon is rather due to the fall in the primary and the secondary sectors, than to the rapid development of the service sector. The case of Hungary illustrates the point. Here employment fell from 5.5 million to 4.4 million, i.e. by over 1 million during the period of 1989–1993. Although the number of employees in the primary sector decreased by more than half (from 986,000 to 431,000) and employment in the secondary sector also dropped (from 2 million to 1.5 million), the number of employees in the tertiary sector remained practically unchanged (even slightly fell from 2.5 million to 2.4 million). That is, the latter's share increased only as a result of the rapid fall in the other two sectors. In most countries, however, the employment share of the service sector with its 40–47% remained below the level of the developed countries.

Unemployment and its structure

In the light of the mentioned developments, it is not surprising that unemployment became very high in almost all countries under consideration. The only exception was the Czech Republic, where open unemployment even fell considerably in 1992 (at a time when in all other countries it increased, or just slightly fell as in Slovakia). As can be seen from Table 3, in all countries, except the Czech Republic, the emergence of mass unemployment coincided, beginning to rise in 1991. This is not surprising in the light of the collapse of the CMEA. In Slovenia, apart from the transition process, the protracted war in the territory of the former Yugoslavia and, in its wake, the collapse of the former trade relations with the other republics explain the rapid increase in the number of people out of work.

Table 3
Registered unemployment rate in the Visegrád countries
and in Slovenia (1989–1994)

Year/period	Czech Republic	Slovakia	Hungary	Poland	Slovenia
1989	–	–	0.5	–	3.2
1990	0.7	1.5	1.0	6.1	5.9
1991	4.1	11.8	8.5	11.4	10.1
1992	2.6	10.4	12.3	13.6	13.4
1993	3.0	12.7	13.4	15.5	15.4
1993 1st quarter	2.9	12.0	12.9	14.2	13.5*
1993 2nd quarter	2.6	12.5	12.7	15.2	14.2*
1994 1st quarter	3.5	14.5**	12.5	16.7	n.a.

Sources: For the Czech Republic and Slovakia: Uldrichová (1993) and *Employment Observatories*, No. 5. December 1993, p. 37. No. 6. October 1994; for Slovenia: Koltay (1994) and Kajzer (1994); for Poland: Karpinska-Mizielinska – Smuga (1993) and Koltay (1994).

* Estimates, based on Kajzer (1994).
** Estimates.
n.a. not available.

Notes:
1. Until 1992 end of period data.
2. Data are not always comparable even within one country, as the method of calculation has changed.

Exceptional tightening of eligibility conditions in January 1992 (including the reduction of the entitlement period from 12 months to 6 months, cutting the level of unemployment benefit, etc.) well explains why the number of registered unemployed fell drastically in Czechoslovakia.[19] It is less understandable, however, how it was possible to keep the level of unemployment well below 10% in the Czech Republic since then and how to explain the widening gap between the unemployment rates of the two republics after the split. It seems that the much higher unemployment in Slovakia actually reflects a common phenomenon in the Central and Eastern European region, namely the high regional fluctuation of unemployment.[20] Those regions, which are specifically adversely affected by the collapse of the CMEA and/or the (often related) transformation process, are inevitably more exposed to unemployment. For example, the Slovakian economy had traditionally been of a more agricultural character than the Czech where industry has much older traditions. The Slovakian industrial structure, having been built up in the communist period, was strongly specialized in the CMEA market.[21] As mentioned, fall in employment in agriculture was particularly pronounced (especially in Hungary but also in Czechoslovakia), in the same way as in the CMEA-oriented sectors of manufacturing. These are the basic reasons that made Slovakia particularly exposed to unemployment.

The same factors are responsible for the diverging labour market outcomes of the different regions within any country of the Central and Eastern European region. For example, in Hungary Borsod-Abaúj-Zemplén county was such a traditional centre of the so-called "socialist industrialization". Here the unemployment rate, at around 20%, stands much higher than the country average. Elsewhere, in some backward areas, where a large number of the population is unskilled, the reasons for unemployment are twofold: first, the main economic activity is agriculture, which has been suffering due to CMEA market losses, a fall in domestic demand, limited foreign demand (because of the European Union's agricultural protectionism) and ownership transformation (for example, transformation of traditional co-operatives). Secondly, these are areas from where labour commuted traditionally to other, more industrialized regions and cities. During the massive dismissals, the unskilled commuters (often Gypsies) are the first to be dismissed. For example, in Szabolcs-Szatmár-Bereg county (in the Northeast), where the rate slightly exceeds 20%, the proportion of Gypsies (10–12%) within the population exceeds double the national average.

Coming back to the issue of unemployment in the Czech Republic, there are obviously other, more specific factors as well contributing to the exceptionally low unemployment in this country. They are as follows:

(1) The restructuring process has not started yet to such an extent as it has for example in Hungary and Poland. It is also reflected in the fact that, thus far, bankruptcy pro-

---

[19] As mentioned, a considerable drop in the activity rate also contributed to lower unemployment. It is to be mentioned that it declined to a greater extent in the Czech Republic than in Slovakia, where the activity rate stood at a lower level initially (see Table 1).

[20] For example, prior to the split of Czechoslovakia in 1992, the minimum regional unemployment rate amounted to 1.4%, whereas the maximum reached 12.6%. At that time in Hungary the respective figures were 7.0% and 18.0%, in Poland 9.0% and 17.4% (*Employment Observatory*, Central and Eastern Europe, No. 3).

[21] In Slovakia, proportionately more people were employed in the metal, electronic, chemical, rubber production and arms industries (*Employment Observatory*, No. 4, May 1993, pp. 11–12). Conversion of the latter causes an especially serious problem.

cedures practically have not started, although the Bankruptcy Law has already come into force.

(2) The geographical location of the country is much more attractive for foreign capital than that of Slovakia. As a consequence, foreign direct investment recently increased, especially in the areas neighbouring Germany.

(3) Despite the delay in privatization, the private sector is expanding, so far mainly through the increase in the number of small private entrepreneurs, relating perhaps to the growing service sector.[22]

(4) The above contributory factors reinforce each other and as a result of low unemployment, more expenses can be spent on active labour market measures.[23]

The sex composition of the unemployed in Central and Eastern Europe is similar to what has been experienced in the OECD countries: women's share is usually higher than men's. There are two exceptions: Hungary, where women's share amounted to only 41% in 1992; and Slovenia, where in 1993 the respective figure was about 44%. In both cases, the recession hit primarily the male-dominated sectors and industries (e.g. agriculture, mining and engineering). In the case of Hungary, the women's lower share can also be attributed to the wide range of maternity provisions.

The general rule of over-representation of unskilled people among the unemployed, as experienced in the OECD countries, also applies to Central and Eastern Europe. However, there seem to be important differences with regard to education. Although by the early 1990s, in the Central and Eastern European countries employment had shifted towards more skilled labour than was the case in the late 1980s, the share of those having vocational training was high among the unemployed in 1991–1992.[24] For example, in November 1992 in Poland, this group was the only one whose share among the unemployed was significantly higher than among the employed persons (40.5% compared to 31.5%). In Hungary, the situation was similar (with the respective figures being 32.8% and 27.2%), but here the share of those with unfinished primary school education was twice as much among the unemployed than among the employed (6.9% versus 3.3%). Those who had only primary schooling were also proportionately more among jobless people than among the employed (the respective figures were 35.7% and 25.6%).[25]

The high share of skilled workers and those with vocational training among the unemployed may be regarded as a specific feature of transitional economies, as this can be associated with the mass release of labour from the state sector and significant changes in the occupational structure of labour demand. Many skills which were previously indispensable for the "socialist industrial structure" are becoming increasingly obsolete.

As regards their future employment opportunities, at first sight the high share of skilled workers among the unemployed may imply some ground for optimism, since in principle they can be retrained easier than the unskilled workers. However, the problem

[22] As early as in 1991, the ratio of Czech employees working in small firms rose by 5%, whereas in Slovakia the respective figure was 1.3% (Svejnar 1993).

[23] By contrast, in other countries (again, mainly in Hungary and Poland) the rapidly increasing expenses for passive labour market policy (in the form of provision of growing unemployment benefits) crowd out the expenditure potentially available for active labour market policy.

[24] See OECD (1992).

[25] These figures are based on LFS (Labour Force Survey) data in both countries. Source: *Employment Observatory*, No. 4, May 1993, pp. 21–22.

with this is twofold. First, amidst the current recession it is not at all clear which skills will be needed in the future. Second, as they were trained in very narrow fields and the level of their general education is low, it is doubtful whether the majority of these workers could be easily retrained.

With respect to the current social structure of the unemployed, a polarization can be observed among them, which is partly associated with the over-representation of skilled workers. In certain occupational categories, especially in the construction industry, skilled workers (e.g. house-painters and bricklayers) certainly have a good chance for employment, especially in the semi-informal or the hidden economy both at home and abroad. For example, in Hungary there are anecdotes about those who are drawing unemployment benefits, and at the same time they take up occasional jobs abroad illegally as skilled workers, earning thus much more than before they were dismissed. For unskilled or semi-skilled workers such opportunities are much more scarce. These workers are more vulnerable, since they are usually employed in the black labour market, where employment conditions are totally different, i.e. much more unfavourable, from those applied in the normal labour market. In addition, there is evidence especially in Hungary and Slovakia that in this the share of vulnerable groups – besides women, also Gypsies – is very high. These facts call for specific measures of a more targeting nature in the field of active labour market policies.

Since the emergence of unemployment, the number of young people out of work has increased considerably. This is partly due to the fact that at the beginning of the transition period eligibility for unemployment benefits was linked to previous working experience in most countries. Thus, drop-outs were excluded from compensation and therefore had no incentive to be registered. At the same time, their growing share among the unemployed can also be associated with the practice of overemployment. Hence, labour hoarding[26] has presumably not ceased to exist. Workers' pressure on hiring and dismissals, just like their bargaining power, depends on many complex factors and it may vary largely across sectors, occupations, regions and countries. Yet, during the first years of the transition, state-owned companies generally preferred "soft methods" of cutting their staff and therefore in a difficult financial position they often resorted to a hiring freeze. Before 1992, this behaviour apparently related to the lack of the Bankruptcy Law, hindering market exit.

So these phenomena, including some hysteresis effects,[27] obviously aggravated young people's entry to the labour market, which is all the more serious, as the growth of the private sector and its absorbing capacity are limited.[28]

As the transformation proceeds, the problem of long-term unemployment, i.e. being without work for more than 12 months, becomes more and more serious. The share of long-term unemployed was already high in 1992 in those countries where mass unemployment emerged, and it reached about 40% by 1994. Although according to the latest available LFS data, in the first half of 1993 the share in Poland dropped (perhaps partly

---

[26] According to Mencinger's estimates, labour hoarding in the former Yugoslavia was around 20% in 1982, and later, by 1988, it had increased to 30%. However, as regards Slovenia, all estimates were considerably lower than in other parts of the former Yugoslavia, although Mencinger put the figure to 15% (i.e. 80,000 hidden unemployed) in the Slovenian industry still in the first half of 1993 (Kajzer 1994, pp. 14–15).

[27] They are due to the power of the insiders as empirical evidence suggests (see Halpern 1994; Commander – Ugaz 1993).

[28] Although empirical evidence from the Hungarian experience suggests that the private sector tends to employ more young people than the state sector does (Bukodi – Harcsa – Reisz 1994).

as a result of growing industrial output), it is still around 35%. However, in most other countries, the number of people without work for more than 12 months continued to rise. For example, in Slovenia in 1993, already 55% of the registered job-seekers were long-term unemployed.

Main dilemmas of labour market policy

Since the beginning of the transition process and the emergence of unemployment, labour market policy has been gradually gaining ground in Central and Eastern Europe. The policy measures basically followed the Western model. The main question is not their relevance (as was raised by some experts), but how to adapt them to the specific needs of a society which had not experienced unemployment over the previous four decades under the conditions of severe financial constraints. These dilemmas mean serious challenges for labour market policies in Central and Eastern Europe as compared to industrialized countries. When unemployment started to rise rapidly, in most of the former socialist countries no institutional network for the realization of labour market policy measures existed (Slovenia is an exception in this respect, but experiences of how to treat mass unemployment were lacking here as well). Although since then the network has been built up in a remarkably short period in all countries, on the one hand, the rapidly growing needs are constantly being confronted with very limited financial means (except for the Czech Republic, thus far); on the other, those experiences which could show how to operate the system as efficiently as possible under the specific conditions of transition and how to make the measures themselves more efficient, are still lacking. The "trial and error" method, which we are currently witnessing, is proving costly. Nevertheless, labour market policy showed remarkable adaptability and flexibility in most cases, as is reflected in its frequent changes.

As mentioned, in almost all the countries, passive labour market policy is currently playing a more important role than the active one, which is reflected in the much higher expenditure for the former (see Table 4). This is not surprising in view of the high level of unemployment. Still it is true that the policy itself does have major impacts on the scale and level of unemployment, as is well known from the literature and OECD experiences. The drastic fall in employment, the collapse of the state sector, the depth of the recession, the high regional fluctuation of unemployment with low labour mobility and other specific features of the transition process, however, have together left a very narrow scope of manoeuvrability for labour market policy in the former socialist countries. The rapid rise in unemployment made it imperative to develop first a symptomatic treatment, i.e. to introduce passive measures quickly in order to avoid major social tensions. In addition, "soft methods", such as early retirement, which were preferred at the beginning in order to cut staff, also implied the spread of passive measures. Moreover, the scope for an active labour market policy is very limited amidst deep recession or serious economic downturn, as shown persuasively by the current experiences of such countries as Sweden (not to mention those severe financial constraints which the Central and Eastern European countries have to face).

So it is understandable that over the past few years, despite the tightened eligibility conditions for unemployment benefits and under the pressure of a growing number of people out of work, the share of passive labour market expenditure has increased at the

Table 4
Composition of public expenditure on labour market programmes between 1991 and 1993 (%)

Programme	Czechoslovakia		Czech Republic	Slovakia	Hungary			Slovenia		Poland[2]		
	1991	1992	1993	1993	1991	1992	1993	1991	1992	1991	1992	1993
Unemployment benefits[3]	78.1	36.2	63.5	73.6	68.4	76.5	72.5	39.4	40.2	81.8	86.0	83.6
Total active measures	21.9	63.8	34.6	19.6	25.7	16.3	18.3	38.3	43.7	15.8	12.4	15.4
Labour market training	1.5	4.4	3.4	6.5	4.4	5.2	8.2	4.0	3.9	0.7	0.8	1.4
Start-up loans	–	–	–	–	10.5	2.6	1.1	–	–	2.9	1.0	1.7
Subsidized employment schemes	14.1	44.3	12.5	13.6	4.5	4.4	3.2	20.7	29.4	3.3	2.0	4.3
Public works	3.2	7.2	7.4	2.9	1.9	2.0	3.2	0.3	1.2	–	0.8	3.8
Youth measures	1.0	4.9	11.3	1.0	0.1	n.a.	n.a.	10.0	9.3	8.8	7.8	4.2
Other	0.0	0.0	1.9	6.8	5.9	7.2	9.2	22.3	16.1	2.4	1.6	1.0
Total expenditure as a percentage of GDP[1]	0.4	0.5	0.2	1.7	1.3	3.0	3.0	1.8	2.6	1.7	2.0	2.8

Sources: For Czechoslovakia: Uldrichová – Karpíšek (1993), p. 19 and *OECD Employment Outlook*, 1992, 1993; for the Czech Republic: Uldrichová (1994); for Slovakia: Otchotnicky (1994); for Slovenia: Drobnic (1994); for Poland: Góra (1994a).

[1] Source: *OECD Employment Outlook*, 1992, 1993. In the case of Czechoslovakia, data refer to the Czech Republic only. (In Slovakia data available only for 1992, when it was much higher than in the Czech Republic, being 2.01%.) In the case of Poland, Góra (1994a).

[2] Own calculations, based on data provided by Góra (1994a).

[3] In the case of the former Czechoslovakia and Poland, data also include other passive measures.

Note: Public works started only from 1992 in Poland.

expense of active measures in all countries, again with the exception of Czechoslovakia.[29] Despite the rising share of unemployment benefit expenditure, the average benefit expenditure per unemployed decreased between 1991 and 1992, as did, even more dramatically, the average active labour market spending per person in all the countries of the region with high unemployment (the former remained constant in Hungary, but the latter drastically decreased here as well).[30]

The legislative framework for labour market policy was established first in Slovenia in 1988/89, then in 1991 in the other countries considered. Under the Acts on Employment, the main principles of financing these measures were laid down. However, in countries with high unemployment, as a consequence of growing financial difficulties, these Acts had to be amended quite frequently.

For example, in Hungary two separate funds exist: the Employment Fund and the Solidarity Fund. Active measures are financed from the former, based entirely on state budget transfers, while the passive ones from the latter, to which the state, employers and employees contribute alike. Under the pressure of growing needs and limited financing capacity of the state due to the high budget deficit, contributions of both the employers and the employees were raised and further changes are planned. In Poland, there is only one fund – the so-called Labour Fund (set up in 1990) – financing both the active and the passive labour market policy; apart from the state, only the employers contribute to it. Until January 1993, labour market policy in Czechoslovakia was financed entirely from the state budget, where a special reserve was separated for this purpose.[31] After the split, when the new states established their own tax reforms and social insurance systems (based on very similar principles), a labour policy funding system similar to the Hungarian one seems to be emerging. There is a compulsory contribution from the part of both the employers and the employees in both new states.[32] This implies that the amount available for labour market policy is much higher in the Czech Republic, where the unemployment rate is low (since the active population is more than twice as much as in the Slovak Republic), despite the fact that the Slovak state's contribution is proportionately greater than that of the Czech state's. Therefore, unless the number of people out of work is also rapidly growing in the Czech Republic, the gap between the two republics will be widening with regard to financing both the passive and the active labour market policy. As a consequence, the financial burden on the Slovak state is likely to become even higher than at present. However, there are some signs showing that certain limits of state support will be introduced in both states,

---

[29] Here in 1991 passive measures accounted for 78% of all labour market expenditures, whereas in the next year this share dropped to 36%.

[30] See Boeri et al. (1993), pp. 2–3.

[31] The much worse labour market situation in Slovakia (i.e. more rapidly growing unemployment) from the very beginning of the transition process is also apparent from the fact that as early as in 1991, the Czech part of the country contributed a much higher share to active labour market policy, as much as 31.5% of its budget reserve, than Slovakia which spent only 15.1% of its reserve, although Slovakia spent more from the federal reserve (obviously because under the pressure of a growing number of unemployed, it needed much more for passive measures). Uldrichová – Karpisek (1993), p. 11.

[32] Even their contribution rate is similar to what was experienced in Hungary when the Solidarity Fund was introduced, as employers' contribution amounts to 3% of the total payroll (the same in Poland) and the employees' pay 1% of pre-tax income, whereas 4% of pre-tax income is defined for self-employed (Uldrichová – Karpisek 1993). In Hungary, contribution rates equalled 1.5% of the payroll for employers and 0.5% of pre-tax wages for employees for the first time, then they were substantially increased to 7% and 2%, respectively. Now there are plans to cut the former to 5%.

especially in the field of active labour market policy. As a result, a shift towards passive measures can be expected, which may also occur as a consequence of higher unemployment (in which case additional funds will be allocated for unemployment compensation from the reserve in the state budget).[33] (On the institutional framework for financing labour market policy measures, see Table 5.)

Table 5
Institutional framework for financing labour market policy measures
in the Visegrád countries and Slovenia

Country	Starting year	Source	Coverage	Contributors	Contribution rates (%)
Czechoslovakia	1991	Special reserve (from the state budget)	A, P	+	–
Czech Republic	1993	Special reserve (from the state budget)	A, P	+++	(a) 1.0 (of gross wage) (b) 3.0
Slovakia	1991	Solidarity Fund	A	+++	(a) 1.5 (b) 5.0
	1993	Employment Fund	A, P	+++	n.a.
Hungary*	1991	Employment Fund	A	+	–
Poland	1991	Labour Fund	A, P	++	(b) 3.0
Slovenia	1988–1989	Employment contributions and other sources of the budget	A, P	+++	(a) 2.35 (b) 2.35

Sources: Drobnic (1994); Góra (1994a); Otchotnicky (1994); Uldrichová (1994).

  A Active measures
  P Passive measures
  + State budget only
 ++ Employers and the state
+++ Employees, employers and the state
 (a) Employees' contribution rate
 (b) Employers' contribution rate
n.a. not available.
* The Employment and the Solidarity Funds are planned to be united in 1996, as it is in Poland. Thus, transfer between the two formally separated funds is expected to become more flexible.

Burden of the state budget to finance labour market policy seems to be large in all Central and Eastern European countries with high unemployment. In 1992 in Poland, the state's contribution to the Labour Fund amounted to 70%; in Hungary, it was more than 45%;[34] in 1993 in Slovakia, it was planned to exceed 50%; and in 1994 in Hungary it approached the Polish level. It is apparent that in view of the high budget deficit, the state budget cannot be burdened further and there are also severe constraints to increase contributions, since the latter may potentially raise labour costs either directly or indirectly, and thus it may discourage job creation – at least in the legal economy. Therefore, I agree with the conclusion which states the importance of improving the effectiveness of expenditures on the labour market policies in Central and Eastern Europe.[35]

[33] See Uldrichová – Karpisek (1993), p. 12.
[34] This figure excludes the amount the state as an employer contributes to the Solidarity Fund (Boeri et al. 1993).
[35] See Boeri et al. (1993).

It must be added, however, that it is not just up to the labour market policy to improve effectiveness, since this issue should be seen in a broader context. For example, highly progressive income taxes and extremely high social security contributions lead to increased tax evasion, which either through illegal employment and/or by under-reporting of wages, keep contributions down and may concurrently encourage abuses of unemployment benefits. Of course, in a general equilibrium, high taxes and social security contributions are justifiable, since it is imperative to generate revenue for the state budget in order to cut the deficit, as well as to improve the social security system. However, thus far policy-makers seem to have ignored these relationships and/or neglected the importance of urgent and major reforms of the social security system. There certainly exist other alternative policy options, e.g. to cut state expenditures and improve the efficiency of the social security system. However, these are beyond the scope of this paper. To sum up: in an economy where the hidden economy is gaining ground, it is more difficult to tackle unemployment problems than in countries where, on the one hand, the hidden economy is relatively small and stable, and on the other, its expansion contributed to the alleviation of social tensions. In this regard, expansion of the hidden economy can be considered as a self-protection of the society against tension. However, if policy-makers want to control the economy and prevent mass impoverishment, this expansion should be prevented, among others, by introducing such a well-elaborated tax reform which is adapted to the specific needs of the economies in transition and is based on the consensus of the society.

Labour market imbalances and rigidities within a macroeconomic context

In assessing recent developments and also in terms of future perspectives, it is important to raise the question to what extent the persistence of high unemployment in Central and Eastern Europe can be attributed to labour market rigidities and what are the chances for a quick elimination of these rigidities. The issue seems to be of especial relevance to the region, since as some experts conclude,[36] the turnover of the unemployment pool is very low compared to the OECD countries. It is true though that the specific circumstances which can explain the low turnover were mainly characteristic of the year 1992. These were, namely: generosity of unemployment compensation, the first appearance of unemployment, the end of the first shock of the collapse of the CMEA, slow private sector development, etc. However, rigidity in the labour markets of Central and Eastern Europe still prevents quick adjustment from the side of labour.

Some of the reasons for the inflexibility, e.g. low labour mobility, companies' reluctance to carry out group dismissals due to high costs and restrictive regulations as well as delayed bankruptcy procedures, have already been discussed. However, the role of wages cannot be ignored either in this respect; and although available empirical evidence is scarce, it is worth taking a closer look at it briefly.

At the early phase of the transition, wage control had been maintained (at least in the state sector) in the Czech Republic, Slovakia, Poland and Hungary in order to curb

---

[36] See Boeri (1993).

inflation and there were also some attempts to freeze wages in Slovenia. However, they did not prove very efficient, so none of them lasted long. In the former four countries, wage control meant that companies were "punished" with high taxes if their wage bill or the average wage per employee exceeded a certain level. Although it is not clear to what extent the restrictive incomes policy was successful in containing wages, within the context of generous unemployment compensation in the early phase of the transition, the policy might have had ambiguous effects specifically in some traditionally low-paid occupations. For example, in Hungary in 1991–1992, when the system of unemployment compensation was relatively generous (i.e. replacement rates were high, being generally more than 60%), an empirical analysis, based on the first wave[37] of the Hungarian Household Panel Survey, found that quite a significant part of the unemployed (one third) would have accepted only such a job where the wage had been even higher than that of the actually employed persons with similar labour market characteristics (i.e. the market wage had been lower than the wage indicated by the unemployed).[38] So as a consequence of low wages (in certain occupations) and generous unemployment benefits at the same time, the incentive to seek a job was not strong, which contributed to the low outflow from unemployment and thus to labour market rigidities. It is true that due to lack of indexation of the benefit, inflation has considerably eroded its value, but real wages also declined due to a fall in output and productivity.

In time, the whole system of unemployment compensation has become tightened everywhere, i.e. replacement rate has been lowered and eligibility conditions have become more stringent, as mentioned. In addition, in some countries, e.g. in Hungary, wage control was lifted and/or the private sector became exempted, as happened in Poland (and with the expansion of the private sector, the latter is of increasing importance). In Slovenia, wage control (freezing) was introduced in March 1993 to stop real wage increase,[39] but it did not last long.

With regard to minimal wage setting, the literature – which is mainly based on experiences of the developed countries – considers it as one of the main factors potentially contributing to the rigidities of the labour market (by discouraging low-wage job creation). Although this may have some relevance to Central and Eastern Europe as well, the reasons are completely different, since inflation is high (on a two-digit level) and indexation of wages does not exist in the former socialist countries. As the minimal wage is usually set once or twice a year through collective bargaining, its real value may erode,[40] unless the frequency of wage setting is linked to inflation, like in Slovenia.[41]

However, as far as wages in general are concerned, the share of non-wage labour costs is high. In Hungary and Poland, the share of social insurance expenditures and other labour taxes exceeded 30% in the early 1990s, which can be considered a serious

[37] It provided information on a representative sample of 2000 families, and the first wave focussed on changes in their characteristics between March 1991 and March 1992.

[38] See Galasi (1993), p. 7.

[39] Real wage increased by 22.3% over the first two years of independence (between October 1991 and October 1993), and real product wages have risen even more, by 33.0% (Kajzer 1994).

[40] As may that of the social provisions, since most of them are linked to the minimal wage.

[41] In Slovenia, minimal wage is usually set twice a year or more often, should the inflation be higher than 5% in two consecutive months (Law on Minimum Wage).

burden on labour costs in international comparison.[42] In addition, in Hungary labour costs have increased sharply over the period 1989–1992. According to Godfrey's estimate, real non-wage labour costs rose by 26%. He concluded rightly that it did not have a favourable impact on labour demand.[43] With regard to this trend, it is not surprising that the three parties (employees, employers and the government) within the tripartite body of the "Council for Reconciliation of Interests" could only agree on the amount of minimal wage with immense difficulties.

Furthermore, the more rapid rise of the Consumer Price Index (CPI) than that of the Producer Price Index (PPI) can also be a source of common concern in Central and Eastern Europe. The wide gap between them[44] and the high labour costs imply not only growing conflicts between employers and employees, but also less hiring (even freezing) from the part of employers, implying, at the same time, also a danger of exerting more pressure for higher wages from the part of "insiders", i.e. those workers who remained in their job after mass dismissals. Empirical evidence seems to support this. In spite of wage control in the early phase of the transition, the insiders' power was manifested in the inelasticity of their wages, despite a rise in unemployment. Presumably, as a consequence of this, an inverse relationship could be observed in the Hungarian industry between relative employment and relative real wages.[45] So wage control seems to have had a limited impact on relative wage adjustment, as the Polish experience also seems to suggest more or less the same effects. In Slovenia, however, the analysis has not supported any relationship between real net wages and employment.[46]

Inflation and inflationary expectations, combined with serious problems of the social security system, also prevent the labour market from becoming more flexible. For example, for those who are not forced to retire, there is no incentive for doing so. On the contrary, due to the quick erosion of the value of pensions, which has been a painful experience over the past decades, older people are discouraged to retire.

It is known that various employment forms, such as part-time employment, characteristic of labour markets in developed countries, are able to make the labour market more flexible. However, its spread cannot be expected in the near future in Central and Eastern Europe, unless the existing wage structure (and perhaps the income tax system) change drastically. Households were (and are) based on two breadwinners and although there have been some proposals to support women to stay at home with a supplementary

---

[42] These figures are percentages of hourly compensation costs for production workers in manufacturing (34.0% in the case of Hungary, and 31.5% in the case of Poland). There are similar values only in Italy (30.6%) and in Sweden (31.3%). For the sake of comparison here are the values for some other countries: Holland 22.6%, Germany 22.8%, Romania 23.1%, Portugal 24%, Spain 24.6%, Czechoslovakia 26.5%, Austria 27.6% and France 28.5%. See Godfrey (1993).

[43] See Godfrey (1993). This is supported by findings of a model, presented by Halpern (1994) which suggested that employment in state companies was negatively associated with real wages between 1989 and 1992 (since this corresponds to theoretical assumptions, Halpern labels the relationship between labour demand and the real product wage as conventional).

[44] As Halpern (1994, p. 68) argued, through the diverging trends in real interest rates of deposits and credits, the wide gap between CPI and PPI has other, indirect and harmful impacts on employment. Rapid growth of CPI, by exerting downward pressure on real interest rates of deposits (making them negative), discourages household savings. At the same time the relatively slow growth of PPI pushes the otherwise high real credit rates even higher, discouraging investment and thus preventing the creation of further jobs.

[45] Employment and wages of a given branch were related to the industrial average (Commander – Ugaz 1993; Halpern 1994).

[46] Although Kajzer (1994, p. 20) noted that more disaggregated data could have offered different results.

income (compensating for the loss in family income due to their dropping out of the labour force), it is unlikely that in economies with such high budget deficits, the idea could be realized.

Conclusions

As a result of the transition process, there was a rapid rise in unemployment. As a reaction to this, labour market institutions have been established and a wide range of measures introduced, but there are several problems which cannot be solved by these, as they are deeply rooted in the economy. One set of problems is associated with the inherited rigidity of the labour market, which is of an extremely high degree (especially compared to the developed countries). Alongside with the artificial preservation of full employment, this derived from narrow, non-transferable skills, low labour mobility, overwhelming dominance of full-time jobs, administrative wage setting by the state, very limited market entry and exit due to dominance of state ownership, bureaucratic co-ordination instead of competition, overwhelming dominance of large companies, very limited self-employment and linkage of social provisions to employment, etc. Although many of these causes of rigidity were abolished, not all of these factors can be eliminated overnight (this is the case, for example, with labour mobility, skills and employment forms). Moreover, the current macroeconomic constraints do not facilitate changes. On the contrary, they sometimes add to the slow adjustment of labour. For example, the private sector's employment-generating capacity is still limited under the conditions of deep recession, high real interest rates for credit and contracting demand. At the same time, in some countries, e.g. in Poland and Hungary, under the pressure of the high budget deficit and the serious financing problems of social security, labour is heavily taxed, which makes employment expensive.

Some scarcely available empirical evidence from Hungary suggests that due to the insiders' power, responsiveness of wages to rising unemployment in the state sector is insignificant. In this respect, the behaviour of the private sector is still unclear, but even with its further expansion (and the parallel contraction of the state sector), no profound change can be expected, mainly due to the existing gap between the supply and the demand patterns of skills.

The other set of problems is connected with the expanding hidden economy. This is all the more important, since it is closely associated with polarization among the un-employed. Those people who have competitive skills on the labour market of the hidden economy are much less vulnerable than those with obsolete skills or without any skill. This has been a source of abuses and therefore the problem calls for much more target-ing measures, and despite all the current difficulties (e.g. the scarce financial resources), active measures should be taken. In addition, there is much to be done to improve the efficiency of active labour market policy measures, for example, by monitoring cost-effectiveness on a regular basis. At the same time, it also seems to be necessary to diversify the active measures; that is, the creation of their institutional framework may seem to be costly now, but it will certainly "pay off" in the medium term and in the long run.

However, broader macroeconomic issues should also be taken into account, since they influence labour market developments to a great extent. This fact does not seem to have been recognized so far and therefore unemployment problems may have been bigger than they should have been, deriving from the transition process itself. For example, when designing a fiscal policy including taxation, the objective of encouraging employment by lowering labour costs should also be considered.

References

Boeri, T. (1993): Labour Market Flows and the Persistence of Unemployment in Central and Eastern Europe. Paper presented at the technical workshop organized by OECD–CCET on The Persistence of Unemployment in Central and Eastern Europe, Paris, 30th September – 2nd October 1993.

Boeri, T. – Keese, M. (1992): From Labour Shortage to Labour Shedding: Labour Markets in Central and Eastern Europe. *Labour Market and Social Policy Occasional Papers,* No. 9, OECD, Paris, 1992.

Boeri, T. – Reutersward, A. – Scarpetta, S. (1993): Unemployment Benefit Systems and Active Labour Market Policies in Central and Eastern Europe: An Overview. Paper presented at the technical workshop organized by OECD–CCET on The Persistence of Unemployment in Central and Eastern Europe, Paris, 30th September – 2nd October 1993.

Bossányi, K. (1993): Kétharmados társadalom. Interjú Kolosi Tamással (A society of two thirds. Interview with Tamás Kolosi). *Társadalmi Szemle,* No. 11.

Bukodi, E. – Harcsa, I. – Reisz, L. (1994): Társadalmi tagozódás, mobilitás (az 1992. évi mobilitásvizsgálat alapján) (Social stratification and mobility – on the basis of the 1992 mobility survey). *Társadalomstatisztikai Közlemények.* Published by the Central Statistical Office, Budapest.

Commander, S. – Ugaz, C. (1993): Hungary Country Study, Employment, Output and Wages in the State Sector: Some Preliminary Analysis. Research Project on Labour Markets in Transitional Socialist Economies. Paper prepared for Stirin Workshop, 16–17 April 1993.

Commission of the European Communities, 1993, Brussels. *Employment Observatory, Central & Eastern Europe,* Nos 3, 4, 5.

Drobnic, S. (1993): Unemployment in Central and Eastern Europe, Privatization and New Organizational Forms. Revised version of a paper prepared for the international conference on Privatization and Socioeconomic Policy in Central and Eastern Europe. Workshop No. 8. Labour Markets and Unemployment. Krakow, Poland, October 18–21.

Drobnic, S. (1994): Employment Policies and Programmes in Slovenia. Paper presented at the Conference on Employment Policy and Labour Market Programmes in Eastern and Central Europe, Budapest, June 2–3.

Employment Barometer, Slovenija 92 – Europe 90, Centre for Welfare Studies: Ljubljana, January, 1993.

Fazekas, K. (1993): A munkanélküliség regionális különbségeinek okairól (On reasons for regional dispersion of unemployment). *Közgazdasági Szemle,* Nos 7–8.

Galasi, P. (1993): Unemployment Benefit, Wages and Job Search Intensity (An Empirical Analysis Based on the First Wave of the Hungarian Household Panel Survey). ILO/Japan Project on Employment Policies for Transition in Hungary, Working Paper No. 8.

Godfrey, M. (1993): Are Hungarian Labour Costs Really so High? Working Paper. ILO/Japan Project on Employment Policies for Transition in Hungary, Budapest.

Góra, M. (1993): Labour Market Policies in Poland. Paper presented at the technical workshop organized by OECD–CCET on The Persistence of Unemployment in Central and Eastern Europe, Paris, 30th September – 2nd October 1993.

Góra, M. (1994a): Role of the State in Labour Market Programmes. Paper presented at the Conference on Employment Policy and Labour Market Programmes in Eastern and Central Europe, Budapest, June 2–3.

Góra, M. (1994b): Labour Market Flows in Economies in Transition: The Case of Poland. In: Eriksson, T. – Leppänen, S. – Tossavainen, P. (eds): Proceedings of the Symposium on Unemployment. Government Institute for Economic Research VATT, Helsinki.

Halpern, L. (1994): A Macroeconomic Framework for Analysis of Unemployment and Development of a Medium-Term Strategy in Hungary. ILO/Japan Project on Employment Policies for Transition in Hungary. Mimeo, Budapest.

Kajzer, A. (1994): Real Wage–Employment Relationship and Unemployment Problems in Transitional Economies – The Case of Slovenia and Hungary. Mimeo, Budapest.

Karpinska-Mizielinska, W. – Smuga, T. (1993): Labour Market in the Process of System Transformation – The Polish Case. Paper presented at the VIIth EADI General Conference, Berlin, 15–18 September 1993.

Köllő, J. (1993): A tulajdoni átalakulás és a munkaerőpiac Magyarországon (Ownership transformation and labour market in Hungary). *Közgazdasági Szemle,* No. 9.

Koltay, J. (1994): Munkanélküliség és foglalkoztatáspolitika Közép- és Kelet-Európában (Unemployment and labour market policy in Central and Eastern Europe). *Közgazdasági Szemle,* No. 2.

Laky, T. (1993): *A munkaerőpiac keresletét és kínálatát alakító folyamatok* (Processes shaping labour demand and supply in Hungary). Munkaügyi Kutatóintézet Országos Munkaügyi Központ, Budapest.

Otchotnicky, P. (1994): Employment Policy in the Slovak Republic. Paper presented at the Conference on Employment Policy and Labour Market Programmes in Eastern and Central Europe, Budapest, June 2–3.

Svejnar, J. (1993): CSFR: A Solid Foundation. In: Portes, R. – Nuti, M. (eds): *Transition in Eastern Europe: Progress Report.* Centre for Economic Policy Research (CEPR), London, 1993.

Uldrichová, V. (1994): Employment Policies and Programmes in the Czech Republic. Paper presented at the Conference on Employment Policy and Labour Market Programmes in Eastern and Central Europe, Budapest, June 2–3.

Uldrichová, V. – Karpisek, Z. (1993): Labour Market Policy in the Former Czech and Slovak Federal Republic. Paper presented at the technical workshop organized by OECD–CCET on The Persistence of Unemployment in Central and Eastern Europe, Paris, 30th September – 2nd October 1993.

Transformation of the financial systems in East-Central Europe

GYÖRGY CSÁKI

Financial services are of predominant importance in the transition period as the "virtual infrastructure of the establishment of the market economy". No part of the financial sector – banks, share and equity markets, insurance companies, financial consulting – is on a fairly acceptable level and it is obvious that in the whole "learning by doing" process of the socio-economic transformation, the development of financial services is a precondition of the overall economic development. From this point of view, the following major obstacles can be described.

Under the mono-banking system, while the national economy was generally deprived of financial services, banking services were also on a fairly poor level, hence there is a general lack of adequate banking services.

There has been an important lack of banking networks, since in the mono-banking/one-tier banking system, the central banks played not simply a great, but a very complex role as well: they had, of course, served as a bank of emission, as an agent of the realization of the state currency monopoly, as a general (and unique!) settlement and clearing centre and as an exclusive account keeper of each economic unit in the country!

Neither private persons, nor the corporate sector had had experiences either in a monetarized economy, up-to-date cash-flow management, or in the use of financial intermediaries.

As far as the starting situation of the emerging new financial systems between 1988 and 1990 in East-Central Europe is concerned, the following points can be mentioned:

• Most of the staff in the new banks had come from the national banks and had been used to the bureaucratic allocation of credits and the concomitant attitude, rather than to making business decisions.

• Credit appraisal methods were rudimentary and therefore did not create a sound basis for credit decisions.

• Although the establishment of a clearing house (giro centre) in Hungary, for example, had been decided years ago, it started operation only in late 1994.

• The internal flow of information in the banks is generally poor.

• Only a few banks had a significant branch network, and even those are still insufficient for the provision of retail services on a large (nationwide) scale. Communications between the branches and the head offices are extremely troublesome, owing to the lack of a well-functioning computer network and the generally poor conditions of data transmission.

• The field in which the banking system lags furthest behind modern requirements even today, is in the method of making personal payments: the population is essentially

89

paid and is paying in cash. Personal account appeared a few years ago, but cheques, debit cards and ATMs (banknote dispensers) although already existing, are still very rare.

• The variety of financial institutions was very limited: apart from the National Savings Bank, there were only commercial banks and commercial bank-like small credit institutions (see: Estrin – Hare – Surányi 1992).

Heritage versus emerging needs

In recent years, the East-Central European countries have introduced banking reforms. Although the scope and depth of these reforms have been different, the separation of central banking and commercial banking functions has proved to be one of their common achievements. In most countries, new commercial banks have been established with certain sectoral or regional specialization. Commercial banks have usually been provided with fairly broad banking authorization. These new commercial banks are mostly owned by the state (in some countries ownership rights are exercised by the central banks). In a few countries, corporate and other entities also became owners. The banking infrastructure has developed gradually. Steps have been or are being taken to organize activities to supervise the new banking institutions. Banking supervisory authorities have already begun their operations. Since the establishment of the two-tier banking system, banks have been free to set their own interest rates for corporate customers. Following the integration of corporate and household banking activities, the interest rate liberalization has been gradually extended to households as well.

Banking systems in East-Central Europe perform the basic functions one would expect in both market and planned economy traditions: i.e. payment, savings and credit functions.

Beside the basic functions, banks provide several specific functions corresponding to the special needs of the economic transformation.

• Banks perform a catalyst function during the privatization of these economies. Banks are expected to provide consulting services and to act as lenders and providers of financial services. Banks also become temporary or ultimate owners in privatized economic units as a result of investment decisions, which may include special techniques, such as domestic debt-equity swaps. Beside financing, banks have a major promotional role towards small private enterprises. Thousands of such enterprises have been established and will need advice in management and help in adapting to a competitive market environment.

• Banks also have a promotional role to facilitate the establishment of security markets. Banks can be major participants on primary markets and can efficiently contribute to the creation of secondary (i.e. OTC – over the counter) markets. Through the latter, financial institutions perform an important liquidity function as well.

• Banks provide a specific risk-covering function during the period of transition. In the absence of well developed financial markets and appropriate institutions, banks play the role of a "general trustee". Off balance sheet transactions, like the provision of sureties and guarantees expand rapidly. The lack of official export credit guarantee institutions also meant until recently a special burden for the banking institutions that are allowed to participate in international trade payments.

Reforming the banking sector

"In western societies bankers are about as popular as lawyers, during recession even less so. Compared with their standing in other cultures, past and present, it is quite an advance."
[*The Economist*, 25 December, 1993, p. 103.]

Important reform steps have been taken in all East-Central European countries in order to establish a fully market-like banking (financial) system.

In Poland, in 1987, the (then monopolistic) household savings bank (PKO) was separated from the Central Bank, and at the beginning of 1989 nine commercial banks were set up in order to take over commercial operations previously performed by branches of the National Bank of Poland. Alongside the newly established commercial banks, the Polish banking system has nowadays two state-owned savings banks, a group of originally state-owned specialized banks and about 90 private banks. Beyond these banks, there are not less than 1600 co-operative banks dealing with rural finance: they are small (having an average equity capital of USD 0.8 million) and are regionally specialized.

State banks are treated preferentially with regard to guarantees on their deposits, but are obliged to pay a fixed rate dividend to the state budget. Licensing rules are liberal, the minimum equity capital required is USD 5 million for Polish owners and USD 6 million for foreign-owned banks. Private banks account for about 5% of the total deposits and about 14% of total lending.

In the Czech Republic, the commercial banking sector is dominated by four "inherited" large and state-owned banks: the former commercial banking arm of the then National Bank of Czechoslovakia, the formerly monopolistic savings bank, a long-term credit institution and the Czech Foreign Trade Bank. These large banks own about 70% of the total banking assets. Nevertheless, in late 1993, there were as much as 47 commercial banks operating in the Czech Republic. This number grew to 56 in mid-1994, prior to the collapse of three Czech commercial banks, including two of the country's biggest ones.

In Slovakia, identical institutions were created in 1990–1991 as in the Czech Republic; after the "velvet revolution" every financial institution was automatically duplicated: there were a Czech Trade Bank and a Slovak Trade Bank, a Czech Industrial Bank and a Slovak Industrial Bank, etc. Nevertheless, important differences in the lending attitudes led Slovakian banks into a much weaker position than their Czech counterparts: Slovakian banks have always been reluctant to push (Slovakian) companies towards serious liquidity problems. Therefore, Slovakian banks had to recognize important losses and, especially in 1992, an important capital flow took place from the Slovak to the Czech banks.

In June 1993, Slovakia had 19 commercial banks, including branches of Czech banks, but the Slovakian banking industry is heavily dominated by three large, formerly state-owned commercial banks. Foreign professional investors (German and Austrian banks, as well as the EBRD – European Bank for Reconstruction and Development) bought shares of Slovak banks in late 1993. The number of Slovakian banks has remained stable in 1994–1995, although some further foreign buy-ins have taken place: especially Raiffeisen increased its equity share in the Tatra Bank. Slovakian banks are supplemented with 10 branches of foreign banks as well as 6 representative offices of major foreign banks.

Slovenia inherited the former Yugoslavia's two-tier banking system: commercial banks run a German-type universal banking practice, being licensed to undertake all kinds of banking services. The Ljubljanska Banka Group owns 14 banks and accounts for almost 90% of the total commercial banking assets: five out of the six largest commercial banks belong to that group. Beyond members of the Ljubljanska Banka Group, there are 18 further commercial banks in Slovenia, most of them having foreign owners too.

Hungary established its two-tier banking system in 1988 in two ways: the three major sectoral credit departments of the central bank became independent commercial banks (viz. the Hungarian Credit Bank, the Trade and Credit Bank, and the Budapest Bank) and the former "special financial institutions" transformed themselves into fully fledged commercial banks. Assets, deposits and loans are heavily concentrated in the above three banks, plus the National Savings Bank and the Hungarian Foreign Trade Bank.

In Hungary, fully foreign owned banks, off-shore banks, joint venture representative offices of foreign banks are also operating: originally they provided services almost exclusively for their domestic clients having business interests in Hungary. One of the major changes in the Hungarian banking industry having taken place in 1994–1995 was that foreign-owned and joint venture banks took over an important market share and could attract especially the best corporate (and even private) clients (see: Várhegyi 1995, pp. 137–138). The Hungarian commercial banks are also German-type universal banks, although their capital market arms (brokerage firms) must be run separately from the headquarters.

Non-performing loans and bank recapitalization

Certainly the most serious obstacle which hinders the banking system from functioning efficiently is the "bad loans" problem. Many banks have large stocks of non-performing loans outstanding to state-owned companies. "For example, at least 26% of the assets of the banking sector in Poland were thought to be non-performing in 1992, while for the former Czechoslovakia and Hungary the corresponding estimates were 21 and 11%. The proportion of bad loans is highest in the state-owned banks. Undercapitalized banks with large exposures to virtually bankrupt large enterprises may be inclined to roll over outstanding loans and to capitalize interest rather than show losses on their balance sheets or force enterprises into bankruptcy or restructuring ... This moral hazard problem undermines the banks' ability to provide an objective assessment of corporate profitability and to ensure that resources are distributed efficiently and argues in favour of a thorough restructuring and recapitalization of the banks. Moreover, until the problem of non-performing loans to enterprises is resolved, the privatization of both banks and enterprises will likely be delayed" (Blommestein – Spencer 1993).

Although experiences are different in the individual countries, two main approaches have emerged: the decentralized approach which relies on the banks themselves to manage the debt restructuring, and the centralized approach which relies on the transfer or sale of non-performing loans to a special state institution. Both approaches have their pros and cons, but regardless of how the "bad loans" problem is handled, *the banks can only be expected to operate on a purely market-oriented basis if they are privatized.*

The problem of bad loans was handled in the most direct way in the former Czechoslovakia. During 1991, the government introduced two separate schemes to tackle this problem. In March 1991, a "Consolidation Bank" was established to take over from the Czechoslovak commercial banks' loans a nominal amount of CKR 110 billion. These loans were all of a particular type of permanently revolving credits which the banks had to issue originally under instruction from the state. On the liabilities side, the Consolidation Bank assumed responsibility for the commercial bank debt owed to the central bank and the savings bank. The transfer of low-interest assets and high-interest liabilities to the Consolidation Bank helped to improve the profitability of the commercial banks. But the scheme did little to address the greater problem of non-performing assets, as the loans that were transferred to the Consolidation Bank were selected on the basis of their terms (i.e. the interest rate) rather than credit-worthiness and payment record.

In a second phase, which was launched in October 1991, the state provided the commercial banks with a capital infusion worth CKR 12 billion and a debt-to-equity conversion worth CKR 38 billion. In the debt-to-equity conversion, the banks would write down claims on companies that were believed to be viable but over-indebted and would, in return, receive bonds in the same nominal amount from the state-owned National Property Fund. The bonds were to be swapped after 5 years for shares in companies whose debt had been written down. The debt-equity swap provided cash-flow relief for both companies and banks, financed by the state, but was aimed at the relatively good companies and did not fundamentally solve the problem of non-performing bank assets. Nevertheless, the problem of non-performing loans has remained and Czech banks try to establish the necessary amount of reserves and widen the spread between lending and deposit rates. Even so, at end-September 1992, 21% of bank loans were classified in the two lowest categories (Blommestein – Spencer 1993). Czech banks seemed to be in a good shape in 1993, "Nonetheless, there are still worrying signs of weakness among Czech banks. The overall level of bad debts in the system is still high – some estimates say one fifth of bank assets looks shaky. Earlier this year [that is: in 1994 – Gy. Cs.] Banka Bohemia, the country's seventh biggest bank, was caught up in a securities scam. And recent annual report of Agrobanka, the fifth biggest, showed that it was technically bankrupt in 1993. The banks' shareholders have since injected more capital to help to solve its problems." (*The Economist,* 27 August, 1994, p. 57.)

The data for Slovakia are rather doubtful: according to official evaluations, no more than 3.2% of the credits of the Slovakian banking system are evaluated as "dubious or questionable". At the same time, the Slovak government is ready to provide compensation worth SLK 4 billion to creditors for their losses. (Ibid. p. 120.)

In Slovenia, the government set up a so-called Bank Rehabilitation Agency in order to tackle the problems of non-performing loans of the Ljubljanska Banka Group: 51% of the needed amount of money will be provided, of which 51% by the Bank Rehabilitation Agency in bonds and cash, 19% will be provided in bonds to compensate the foreign currency claims of the Ljubljanska Banka at the National Bank of Yugoslavia. The remaining 30% will be provided as credit. (Ibid. p. 125.)

In Poland, an indirect "recapitalization" has taken place: according to the Company and Bank Restructuring Act, seven out of the nine largest commercial banks, as well as the major savings banks and the Bank of Agriculture and Food Economy have been allowed to receive financial injection in form of state bonds. The initial amount of recapitalization was not less than PLZ 21 trillion, but the process has not been completed yet. All the interested banks were obliged to establish and run special "work-out departments" for tackling the problems of those companies which have, according to the auditors of the bank, sub-standard or non-performing loans. Companies must prepare a reorganization plan and present it to the work-out department, and if the reorganization plan is accepted, the bank will decide how the reorganization would actually take place. The reorganization scheme could include partial write-offs, debt rescheduling, or debt-equity swaps. The banks themselves very rarely provide direct financial help (including fresh money). If the bank does not accept the reorganization plan, it will propose final liquidation. Nevertheless, "for the banking sector as a whole, the average share of bad assets rose from 16% of total credit in 1991 to 26% in 1992" (OECD, 1993). At the end of 1992, half of the bad loans were claimed by the nine large state-owned commercial banks. Nevertheless, bail-outs of bad debts in Poland were hampered (or even stopped) by the breakdown of the privatization process: after the political rows related to the very first major bank privatization (that of the Bank Slaski), no further bank privatization has taken place in Poland. "The Government now says it wants to consolidate banks before privatising them, on the grounds that the regional banks need to be replaced by stronger national groupings. But this process is fraught with difficulties, not least the question of how to price a newly merged bank. More ominous is the possibility that Polish Government is no longer keen to privatise the banks at all." (*The Economist,* 27 August, 1994, p. 58.)

In Hungary, a direct, centrally managed recapitalization consisting of three consecutive phases has taken place. In 1992, a loan consolidation scheme was realized, under which commercial banks could swap their bad loans (of about HUF 114 billion) to state bonds on a discount value of 50–80%. In 1993, in the framework of a bank consolidation programme, commercial banks received a capital infusion – in form of direct capital increase of about HUF 220 billion – in order to have an at least non-negative capital adequacy ratio. The total amount of non-performing loans represented 1.8% of the total credit outstanding at end-1992, 4.5% at end-1993, while it decreased to 3.5% at end-1994 due to the write-off of some of the non-performing loans. In 1994, as much as 55 large state-owned companies were planned to be reorganized, similarly to the above-described Polish practice. The estimated amount of total corporate debts of the above 55 companies was about HUF 80 billion. Nevertheless, the overall assessment of the Hungarian loan–bank–debtors consolidation schemes is rather poor: "Hungary has done the worst job of cleaning out its banks' Augean stables. (...) Altogether Hungary has spent a total of over [USD] 3 billion bailing out its banks, the equivalent of 10% of the country's GDP. In the process, the government has doubled its domestic debt. Yet it has little to show efforts. Almost all of the country's biggest banks are still in state hands: only the Foreign Trade Bank has been partially privatised." (*The Economist,* 27 August, 1994, p. 57.)

As Table 1 shows it clearly (Buch 1994), the amount and share of non-performing loans were permanently increasing, therefore, the problem of bad loans was not simply a question of heritage. The high level of non-performing loans has reflected the high level of non-performing corporate assets, the generally low performance of the national economy. Banks are reluctant to break relations with non-performing firms because: first, account-keeping can be lucrative for them, even for firms which have important amounts of non-performing loans; second, in the most frequent case, state-owned banks are keeping non-performing loans of state-owned firms, therefore, privatization – including that of the large commercial banks – will/would be the only possible solution to eliminate the non-performing loans.

Table 1
Non-performing loans in East-Central Europe

	Czechoslovakia	Hungary	Poland
Amount of non-performing loans	1992: CKR 130 billion	1987: HUF 3 billion	1991: PLZ 30.5 trillion
out of which:		1990: HUF 43 billion	1992: PLZ 60.8 trillion
suspicious	55 billion	1992: HUF 265 billion	1993 (March):
non-performing	75 billion	1993 (March):	PLZ 85.1 trillion
		HUF 194.3 billion	
out of which:			
sub-average	38.4 billion		
doubtful	67.5 billion		
bad	88.4 billion		
Percentage of all banking loans	1987: 0.3%	1991: 7%	
Total assets	1990: 2.6%	1992: 38%	1991: 16%
	1992: 11% of	1993: 30%	1993: 32%
	all banks	Non state-owned	
	15% of four	1990: 10%	
	large, state-	1991: 20%	
	owned	1993: 30–60%	

Source: central bank statistics.

Bank privatization

If the cleaning up of bank portfolios and/or the recapitalization of banks will not be accompanied by a radical change in management practices, the current poor lending practices will likely continue. In East-Central Europe, where the state is still by far the greatest owner, it may be desirable to privatize banks with the shortest possible delay Privatization is probably the quickest way to bring about the deep management changes necessary to give the banks independence from the government as well as to break the banks' subservient role towards the public sector.

In Poland, the bank privatization strategy was fixed in 1991 as follows:

• To attract major Western commercial banks to become strategic partners for Polish banks through the sale of a minority equity stake. The strategic partner would be encouraged to enhance the value of its investment by becoming actively involved in the management of the Polish bank.

• To retain a residual shareholding in the hands of the State Treasury, represented by the Minister of Finance. This residual shareholding would probably carry special rights in certain extraordinary situations, particularly if a change of the controlling stake is involved.

• To make available to its employees at half price up to 20% of a bank's shares offered to outside investors.

• To sell the remaining shares on the Polish market in a public offering to both retail and institutional investors.

The very first bank privatization in Poland was the easiest one: the relatively small Export Development Bank was established in 1987, it had no bad loans and had a relatively high level of managerial practice. Nevertheless, the Export Development Bank was not attractive enough to foreign strategic investors. Therefore, the government changed its mind and privatized the Export Development Bank in July 1992 fully on the domestic market. Table 2 shows the ownership structure of the Export Development Bank in percentages.

Table 2
Ownership structure of the Polish Export Development Bank (%)

	Prior to privatization	After privatization
Ministry of Foreign Economic Relations	41.0	13.5
Ministry of Finance	10.0	–
National Bank of Poland	10.0	–
Three state-owned banks	10.0	–
Private and public trade companies	29.0	39.0
Public	–	37.5
Employees	–	10.0

Source: OECD, 1993, p. 133.

The offer for the public (37.5%) was divided into two tranches: a Large Investor Tranche (22.5%) for those who buy more than 300 shares and a Small Investor Tranche (15%).

The offer price was PLZ 155,000, which is equal to about USD 10.5 per share. This offer price valued the bank at approximately PLZ 310 billion compared to the book value of PLZ 600 billion as of December 31, 1991. The most significant investor in the Large Investors Tranche was an Austrian bank, which ended up acquiring 5% of the Export Development Bank. Since this investment did not occur through a negotiated transaction, no special rights or responsibilities are attached to this stake.

The second important bank privatization in Poland turned out to be "too successful": after the Dutch ING had bought a 25.9% stake of the Bank Slaski for USD 57.1 million on issue price of PLZ 500,000 per share, 30% was publicly offered on the Warsaw Stock Exchange and share prices soared on the first day of trading to PLZ 6.7 million (USD 310) per share. A day later, "Slaski turnover accounted for a mere 0.35% of the banks equity" (*The Financial Times,* January 26, 1994, p. 16). It was "too much" for the government: the deputy finance minister Stefan Kawalec, having been responsible for the financial institutions (banks and insurance companies as well) since 1989, was immediately dismissed. This political row has hampered further bank privatization until now.

In the former Czechoslovakia, 50% of each commercial bank was publicly offered under the voucher privatization scheme. Furthermore, equities – blue chips – of three banks (Ceska Sporitelna, Koresni Banka and Zivnotenska Banka) have been heavily traded on the Prague Stock Exchange. In the opinion of some experts, the "Prague Stock Exchange boom" was largely due to the above bank equities, as well as to four further corporate stocks. According to Austrian investment experts, 80% of the trade on the Czech stock market is made by foreigners. Nevertheless, the state run loan consolidation in the early stage of the transition, and the important capital injection by the state together with the voucher privatization helped to solve the original stock problems of the Czech commercial banks effectively and made the establishment of new banks fairly attractive. At the same time, "the Czech authorities have been reluctant to encourage substantial foreign involvement in banking" (Marrese 1994, p. 15). Since through the voucher privatization the asset management is concentrated by the large investment funds, mostly owned by state-owned banks or by banks with a major state ownership, the Czech banking system is not simply highly concentrated, but is concentrated mainly through the state-owned banks.

An especially interesting foreign buy-in was the takeover of Interbanka, a relatively small commercial bank, by a Hungarian consortium initially led by Magyar Hitelbank (Hungarian Credit Bank), the largest Hungarian commercial bank (which is still in state ownership). Interbanka has a statutory capital of CKR 300 million, is operating as a universal bank, but intends to shift toward trade financing, especially between the Czech Republic, the Slovak Republic and Hungary. Since then, the "Első Hazai Faktorház" (First Domestic Factoring House) and PVL Leasing, both owned by the same three Hungarian private persons, have become the majority shareholders of Interbanka. Interbanka is 62% owner of InterLeasing (the minority owner is the above-mentioned PVL Leasing), full owner of the InterCoupon Investment Fund and co-owner of Czech Insurance. Therefore, Interbanka is a real financial holding with a fairly wide range of activities (privatization, brokerage, insurance, trade financing and traditional commercial banking activities). (*Heti Világgazdaság,* May 6, 1994, pp. 125–126.)

The Slovak Republic has "inherited" banks that were privatized under the voucher privatization scheme in the former Czechoslovakia. Austrian banks have been keen to buy stakes in Slovakian banks. The first one was the Raiffeisen Zentralbank which in November 1990 bought a 33.75% stake in Tatra Banka (which had, at that time, SLK 402 million of statutory capital). In 1992, the Österreichische Volksbank fully bought the Ludova Banka which had SLK 300 million of statutory capital. In early 1994, the Vienna-based Girocredit bought a 10% stake of the Istrobanka accompanied with an option for further 24% stake. Istrobanka had a statutory capital of SLK 800 million and one of its owners is Slovakia's largest insurance company which is strategically related to the bank. In the meantime, Raiffeisen increased its ownership to 45% in Tatra Banka, and the EBRD also made a 15% buy-in in 1993. The Raiffeisen Zentralbank bought further 20% in late February 1994. Further Austrian banks are also likely to open up new businesses in Bratislava: Creditanstalt has opened a branch with SLK 300 million statutory capital and 40 employees and Bank Austria has also officially expressed its plan to establish its affiliate in Bratislava.

Other foreign institutions are also present in Slovakia: many western European banks were forced "to duplicate" their Prague office after the separation. Some others think "it is better to be second in Bratislava than twenty-seventh in Prague ...". Nevertheless, Slovak banks continue to face difficulties in modernizing their operations and introducing new technologies and services. To resolve these problems is not simply a question of the number of banks. Therefore, according to the senior deputy chairman of the largest commercial bank in Slovakia, "The greatest need is for new capital, not more banks" (Blommestein 1993/94).

In Hungary, plans for the privatization of major banks have been on the agenda since as early as 1989 – without having been realized so far. Nevertheless, shares of some – even major – banks are traded on the OTC markets: while setting up a two-tier banking system, a strange cross-ownership came about, since large state-owned companies became shareholders of their account-keeping bank and vice versa. Some bank shares had been sold (probably in 1989–1990) before the State Property Agency or the State Asset

97

Management Company could take over. Some bank shares were "swapped" for Compensation Vouchers. Furthermore, some foreign professional investors bought in into small and medium-sized Hungarian banks. It happened mostly in 1990–1991, when major tax allowances attracted foreign banks. Since then, foreign banks have seemed to prefer establishing a fully owned affiliate or branch – in order to "accompany their domestic clients to Hungary". Hungarian authorities hoped that two out of the five large state-owned commercial banks – the Hungarian Foreign Trade Bank and the Budapest Bank – would be privatized in 1994. In fact, the Hungarian Foreign Trade Bank was privatized in early 1994: EBRD bought 10% and Bayerische Landesbank bought 25%. It was the first case when a major commercial bank was privatized. Nevertheless, one must know that the Hungarian Foreign Trade Bank, as the inheritor of the state monopoly of all banking operations related to foreign trade, had no bad loans, had no doubtful (and/or risky) clients and was the "smallest big bank" in Hungary. The privatization of the Budapest Bank failed in early 1995: after a closed invitation for bids, Credit Suisse was designated as the first, ING as second and Allied Irish as third. The latter declined its bid when it realized that no real tender would take place, the first withdrew its bid after a two months' long due diligence, while ING did the same – without due diligence. It was, of course, a sensitive loss of prestige for Hungary – especially because it happened in a period when privatization in Hungary faced several difficulties. Although the Budapest Bank is permanently declared to be "ready for privatization", it is doubtful when, how and with whom it would be privatized. In the meantime, two other large state-owned commercial banks have been obliged to execute an important (seven- to tenfold) capital decrease and their privatization is unlikely to take place in the coming two or three years.

However, there was also a successful bank privatization in Hungary in mid-1995: 20% of the shares of the largest Hungarian bank, the National Savings Bank were given to the two social security funds, 20% were sold to foreign institutional investors on a 120% share price (no more than 2.5% were allowed to be bought by each single institutional investor) and the same amount was sold at the same share price on the Budapest Stock Exchange. A special method of privatization was used in the case of Postabank: the HUF 6.5 billion worth equity capital was increased through a public offer with not less than HUF 9 billion. Foreign ownership increased from 20 to 40%, (held by two Austrian commercial banks), hence, (indirect) state ownership decreased to an insignificant level.

How to promote the emerging private sector

"Eastern European banks stand accused of ignoring the
private sector.
Blame instead their governments, and the high risk of lending."
[*The Economist,* 27 November, 1993, p. 85.]

However dynamically banking systems can develop, however relatively complete the regulatory framework of the financial sector – for example, in Hungary – can be, the most harmful backwardness is certainly lying in the poor promotion and support of the emerging private sector.

On the one hand, the banking sector is undercapitalized all over East-Central Europe. Banks are full of bad loans, inflation is rather high, and because of the heavy budget deficit, the state budget collects as much savings as possible. Therefore, banks have a fairly large margin between interests on loans and deposits and can generate a nice return on Treasury Bills. On the other hand, the emerging private sector, especially the new ventures, are doubtful borrowers, since they do not have a credit record, they have not enough capital and generally intend to build their new business mostly upon borrowed resources, they are generally inexperienced in business, etc. Therefore, nowadays it is extremely risky to provide loans to new, mostly small and medium-sized companies. Due to the above risks, banks require high collateral (150–200%) and immobile collateral can be taken into account at a 70% discount value, spreads are high, maturities are as low as possible, etc. In Hungary, banks are reluctant to take part in providing special credit facilities, which would promote the emerging private sector, because of the relatively low margins.

While analysing risk sharing in crediting, banks are claimed to act as business organizations which must make strict cost-benefit and risk-return on capital analysis when making decisions. Banks and companies are equal economic partners – at least according to the microeconomics manuals. But in a transitory economy, the emerging private sector, both the newly born and the privatized companies, must be promoted and supported with a complex set of regulatory and financial allowances, including favourable borrowing possibilities. Hungarian banks, for example, try to operate as commercial banks and their credit practice is that of the commercial banks, while neither investment banks nor venture capital are operating on the Hungarian market. Under such circumstances, the "better" and mostly foreign-owned banks can choose their clients: small and medium-sized foreign and joint venture banks are financing the "best" (and mostly foreign-owned and/or joint venture) Hungarian companies, while the "rest of the banks" must/might finance the "rest of the companies". This is a relevant phenomenon for each of the East-Central European transition economies.

Capital market development

"First, there was the timing of the market's launch, amid sweeping economic change and a deep recession. It was like launching a stock market in the middle of the US Great Depression."
[*Euromoney*, March 1993, p. 135.]

Emerging capital markets in East-Central Europe have, potentially, several important roles to play in the overall transformation process, including: facilitating the process of privatization; providing risk capital or long-term debt finance for restructuring and expansion; providing a mechanism for corporate control; and providing domestic and foreign savers (including institutional investors) with instruments to diversify their portfolios, thereby encouraging savings and the mobilization of funds.

There are stock markets in all of the East-Central European countries, including the Budapest Stock Exchange, the Warsaw Stock Exchange, the Prague Stock Exchange, the Bratislava Stock Exchange and the Ljubljana Stock Exchange.

The establishment/building of the capital market is a hard and time-consuming task and it should not be forgotten that these countries never had much experience with dynamic and active stock markets. In mid-1995 there were 42 corporate shares listed on the Budapest Stock Exchange, 26 on the Warsaw Stock Exchange and 10 on the Ljubljana Stock Exchange. Treasury Bills, Compensation and Privatization Vouchers are playing a predominant role. Nevertheless, 1993 (especially the second half of the year) brought a surprising boom on the emerging stock markets of East-Central Europe: the 1993 change in dollars was 791% in Warsaw, 96% in Prague and 24% in Budapest, while the P/E (price–earnings) ratio was equal to 30 in Warsaw, 17 in Prague and 16 in Budapest.

It was voucher privatization that fuelled the Prague Stock Exchange: although it was established in April 1993, and the very first business day took place in June, there are papers of as much as 650 privatized companies traded, out of which only three were really listed in late 1993. There are 269 investment funds trading with shares, but the concentration is extremely high: "Robert Finney, a lawyer with Denton Hall Burgin & Warrens, which was advising the Czech Republic on mass privatization, confirms that government officials are very worried about the concentration of power in the hand of funds. After the first wave, almost 70% of the shares were controlled by the top 14 funds" (Meth-Cohn 1993). These funds are reluctant to sell: the nominal value of CKR 1000 is double the market prices, therefore the boom was greater in the number of papers than in the share prices. Nevertheless, foreign purchases of Czech bonds and equities surged after autumn 1993 based on optimism about the economic and political perspectives of the Czech Republic. Almost USD 2 billion in foreign portfolio investment are estimated to have flowed to Prague since the stock market was opened.

In 1993, Warsaw was one of the most dynamically developed "emerging markets" with its 11-fold stock market rise in zloty terms. Until early 1993 Polish stocks were dull. The index of all Polish stocks, launched at 1000 on April 16, 1991, had ducked as low as 635 in 1992, then had evened out and drifted higher on rising volume. In mid-1993 "The index stood at a little more than 1000 when the market absorbed three bits of good news: an austerity budget, a 600 points fall in interest rates, and a debt deal with the International Monetary Fund. Suddenly, there were more buyers than shares" (Copeland 1993b). Domestic investors know that the inflation is at 37% a year, dollar appreciates at about 30% a year, bank accounts yield 33% a month – but share prices on the Warsaw Stock Exchange sometimes climb up by 30% in one week. At the end of July, there were 102,000 investors in Poland with the number growing by 5000 a month. Beyond increasing domestic demand, investment activity in Warsaw has been generated also through western government-sponsored funds, such as the USD 300 million Polish–American Enterprise Fund. This has channelled loans and equity to small and medium-sized business, and during 1993 contributed USD 50 million to the USD 150 million Polish Private Equity Fund for equity investment, some of which were in companies preparing for eventual stock market flotation.

Official estimates put foreign ownership of stock at about 30% of the Warsaw Stock Exchange's current USD 2.9 billion capitalization. Nevertheless, the Polish government has failed to take advantage of the growth in demand for shares on the Warsaw Stock Exchange for speeding up the privatization of state-owned companies. It offered no more than a handful for sale through a public offering in late 1993. But private companies have been equally reluctant to come to the market to raise funds through fresh equity issues. The growing domestic interest and the increasing foreign investments resulted in the first major boom on the Warsaw Stock Exchange in 1993.

The Budapest Stock Exchange was the first in the region opened up for business in 1990, but the dynamism of its development has been lower than expected. "Exaggerated expectations dominated the Budapest Stock Exchange in the year of opening, as did the unsuccessful introductions in 1991. In 1992, the Budapest Stock Exchange became a market for Treasury Bills and the share market was almost dead, therefore, the disappointment was general. Nevertheless, there were some encouraging signs at the end of 1992: the successful privatization of the Danubius Hotel and Spa Ltd. as well as the Pick Ltd. were the hopeful signs that privatization and capital market building would support each other as it had been expected earlier" (Hardy 1994).

In 1993 the yearly turnover of the Budapest Stock Exchange was about HUF 18 billion – which is less than a tenth of the increase of current private savings (HUF 212 billion). In 1994, the yearly turnover was equal to HUF 21.6 billion (USD 270 million), which represented no more than HUF 1.3 billion market capitalization. The really new phenomenon of the emerging stock markets of East-Central Europe was the dynamically growing foreign investment interest. Since interest rates as well as return on state bonds and Treasury Bills on the major western markets are fairly low, the interest of institutional investors turned towards the "emerging markets". The same happened in 1989–1990, when Latin-American, Spanish and Southeast Asian stock markets attracted a huge amount of capital inflow. Many fund managers turned from bonds to shares and, in order to diversify their investment portfolio, they have become interested in investing more and more on the emerging markets of East-Central Europe. Hungarian papers first attracted foreign institutional investors on the Vienna Stock Exchange as well as in the German OTC-market. Then demand shifted slowly to the same shares on the Budapest Stock Exchange and, later on, it led to a general boom of the whole Budapest Stock Exchange. Due to the relatively low turnover on the Budapest Stock Exchange, 4–5 important investors can fuel the whole market – as it happened in January 1994.

Special foreign (or foreign led) investment funds are also active on the emerging markets of East-Central Europe: Creditanstalt Bankverein from Vienna runs a USD 120 million investment fund in Prague, Pioneer Group Inc. from Boston runs the USD 400 million American-style open-end mutual fund in Warsaw and Pioneer First Polish Trust has attracted as much as 150,000 local investors who amounted up an average USD 2500 apiece to get on Board (*Business Week,* January 17, 1994, p. 37).

Institutional investors welcomed the new CSFB (Credit Swiss First Boston) Fund for East-Central European investments, since fund managers are optimistic about the long-term prospects for East-Central European stock exchanges, given the outlook for a solid macroeconomic development and successful modernization – despite the current economic difficulties and the recent share performances. The immediate press coverage was a welcoming one, quoting optimistic reflections from fund managers. They have stated that there will be further breaks in performance from time to time, because of the relatively small extent of the market, but certainly for 1994 and well into the next years the growing interest in East-Central Europe will remain. What is even more important: institutional investors were keen to buy shares of USD 140 million worth in a couple of days. The importance of the growing interest of mutual and/or investment funds is a crucial issue: it can be the first sign of a real breakthrough if well established investment funds invest in East-Central Europe on a long-term basis. Nevertheless, 1994 and the first half of 1995 have not seen any major breakthrough on the emerging markets of East-Central Europe: the USD 270 million in Budapest, 1.4 billion in Prague and 5.4 billion in Warsaw as yearly turnover of the stock markets are not sufficient to fuel investment and growth.

Nevertheless, nobody should have *illusions* about the future role of East-Central European stock exchanges. There are several important factors which hinder the development of an Anglo–Saxon-type capital market in this region. First, there is a major lack of capital, there is no tradition and experience in capital market activities, market knowledge is inadequate, there are no major institutional investors (except the Investment Funds in the Czech Republic), the current (and underdeveloped) accounting and auditing systems and methods make asset/share evaluation uncertain, etc. Second, current macroeconomic and monetary situations and policies are not supportive for the stock exchanges – high inflation, high interest rates, the overwhelming role of Treasury Bills, the slow progress of privatization, the emergence of German-type universal banks are also very much against both the quick development of stock exchanges and their predominant role on the capital markets.

Summary – perspectives

1. The privatization of the large commercial banks is the most important issue in the reform of the financial system in East-Central Europe. Regardless of all the major problems – bad loans, poor level of settlements, lack of really operating networks, etc. – banks can only operate on a purely market-oriented basis if they are privatized. In view of the current economic and financial climate in both the East-Central European and the OECD countries, the options for privatizing the banks in East-Central Europe are limited. The large state-owned banks are clearly not ready for privatization through flotation on a stock exchange. Apart from mass privatization programmes, the only other viable strategy in the short term is probably a trade sale of all or part of the equity to a strategic investor or group of investors. And, in view of the limited availability of domestic funds, the investor would be most likely foreign. Although, by buying large state-owned commercial banks, foreign strategic investors could buy a good branch network, with a large and generally diversified customer basis, relatively low wages and a wider than general margin, it is rather doubtful whether it is effective enough or even useful for them.

2. As far as the current activities of foreign banks are concerned: "Despite the rapid growth in the number of banks, effective competition in the core retail banking sectors has not developed: and it may take a considerable time for this to happen. Foreign banks, in particular, appear to be primarily interested in wholesale banking and the development of 'niche' activities where their greater technical sophistication and international connections offer the prospects of relatively high earnings; retail banking, with its much greater need for 'up front' investment in banking infrastructure, has thus far been of little interest to these banks" (Westlake 1992). Foreign banks are ready to accompany their domestic clients to East-Central Europe, but have no real interest to take part in the complicated reform process of the East-Central European countries. This is the real cause of their reluctance to buy all or part of the large state-owned East-Central European commercial banks.

3. In the end, governments will be obliged to use fiscal resources for cleaning up bank portfolios and also those major state-owned companies which they would like to keep in operation – either for future privatization or for permanent state ownership. Due to budgetary obstacles, it will not be an easy task and will take a long time. Therefore, bank reorganization will be contradictory and relatively slow – at least in the short term. Large state-owned commercial banks must improve their performance on their own – with important state assistance.

4. Entrepreneurs need equity and long-term credit the most. However, banks are ill-equipped in this respect and reluctant to supply these. They cannot lend long term, since the market will not extend them credit for much more than a year. It will remain one of the greatest economic – and even political – problems and will certainly not be solved without investment banking and venture capital.

5. Capital markets in formerly planned economies have, potentially, a number of important roles to play in the transformation process, including: facilitating the process of privatization; providing risk capital or long-term debt finance for restructuring and expansion; providing a mechanism for non-inflationary finance for the government; providing mechanisms for corporate control; and providing domestic and foreign savers (including institutional investors) with instruments to diversify their portfolios, thereby encouraging savings and the mobilization of funds.

Unfortunately, existing capital markets in the former centrally planned economies are ill-equipped to perform these tasks in the immediate future (Blommestein – Spencer 1993).

The Warsaw, Prague and Budapest stock markets are unlikely to play a really decisive role. One must not have illusions: the share of private/individual shareholders is diminishing on almost all stock exchanges, it is less than 30% in Paris and no more than 20% in London! There are much more individual shareholders than a decade ago, but the share of privately owned stock is decreasing (while that of institutional investors is booming). In East-Central Europe, one had better realize: "Why has popular capitalism not taken root? Largely, because it was an unrealistic dream. Privatization was never going to create an army of active shareholders. Individual direct investment is not worthwhile without specialized knowledge and the cash to build diversified portfolios. Most new shareholders lack both investment skills and money. Better to pool the risk and leave decisions to professional managers by investing through the institutions. A share-owning democracy is a neat political phrase – but the market tells against it" (*The Economist,* 6 December, 1993).

The future of East-Central European stock markets depends largely on foreign investors: nowadays, there is a certain "flow" towards emerging markets in East-Central Europe. It is a question, however, whether e.g. Austrian investment funds are looking for short-term speculation profits or long-term investment possibilities. This will decide the future of the East-Central European stock markets.

References

Blommestein, H. J. (1993/1994): Banks in the East: Path to privatization. The *OECD Observer,* December/January.
Blommestein, H. J. – Spencer, M. G. (1993): The Role of Financial Institutions in the Transition to a Market Economy. IMF Working Paper, International Monetary Fund, Washington, D.C., October 1993.

Buch, C. M. (1994): Insolvency Costs and Incomplete Information in Commercial Banks – Implications for Financial Reform in Eastern Europe. Kiel Working Paper No. 616.

Copeland, H. (1993a): Local Banks Stand up to Foreign Competition. *Euromoney,* December.

Copeland, H. (1993b): Warsaw Roars while Budapest Soars. *Euromoney,* July.

Csáki, Gy. (1993): Recent Improvements of the Hungarian Banking System. Working paper No. 25. Institute for World Economics, Budapest.

Estrin, S. – Hare, P. – Surányi, M. (1992): Banking in Transition: Development and Current Problems in Hungary. *Soviet Studies,* Vol. 44, No. 5.

Foreign Tidal Wave Hits Eastern Bourses. *The Financial Times,* February 4, 1994.

Go East, Young Man – and Play the Market. *Business Week,* January 17, 1994.

Hardy, I. (1994): Felfűtött részvénypiac (Heated share and equity markets). *Figyelő,* January 27.

Makay, L. (1994): Egy boom anatómiája (The anatomy of a boom). *Bank & Tőzsde,* February 14.

Marsh, D. – Denton, N. (1994): USD 200 million East European Fund Launched. *The Financial Times, February 4.*

Marrese, M. (1994): Banking Sector Reform in Central and Eastern Europe. International Monetary Fund, Washington, D.C., 1994.

Meth-Cohn, D. (1993): Investment Funds: Second Thoughts. *Business Central Europe,* July–August.

One Little Piggy Went to Market – but Starved. *The Economist,* 27 November, 1993.

Relieving Central Europe's Banks of Their Burdens. *The Economist,* 27 August, 1994.

Share ownership: Risk Aversion. *The Economist,* 6 December, 1993.

Szántó, A.: Magyar bank Csehországban: A pontosan tervezett jövő (Hungarian bank in the Czech Republic: the punctually designed future). *Heti Világgazdaság,* May 6, 1994.

Transformation of the Banking System: Portfolio Restructuring, Privatisation and the Payment System. OECD, Paris, 1993.

Várhegyi, É. (1995): *Bankok versenyben* (Competing banks). Pénzügykutató Rt., Budapest.

Westlake, M. (1992): Can the Banks Fly? *The Banker,* September.

Foreign direct investments in the countries of the "Visegrád group"

ISTVÁN MÁDI

Transforming economies of East-Central Europe suffer from serious deficiencies that must be overcome if the aim is to catch up with the advanced western countries and to utilize the region's historical potentials. These deficiencies are as follows: (1) The capital stock gap, which is due to a chronic shortage of capital and to the capital becoming obsolescent in the course of the transformation. (2) The technology gap, which is closely linked to the lack of innovative firms and competition on the one hand, and to the lack of intracompany technology flows and cross-licensing that dominate international technology trade, on the other. (3) Lack of entrepreneurship, which is a consequence of the totalitarian socialist period.

Foreign direct investments (FDI) are of predominant importance in the transition period, since the massive inflow of foreign direct investments can play a decisive role in filling the capital and technology gap, and in creating a market-conform business environment. Foreign investors transfer not only capital and technology, but also knowledge of modern business behaviour and techniques. Furthermore, foreign direct investments can contribute to economic growth via the increasing capital and technology spillovers. Economic growth is vitally important for sustaining transformation, because privatization and modernization are inevitably accompanied by mass unemployment and unprecedented social tensions. These undesired phenomena must be alleviated, otherwise social disturbances could derail transformation.

Recent trends in foreign direct investment flow to the "Visegrád group"

Investment flows and stocks

During the socialist period, when the private sector of the Central and East European economies was severely restricted and essentially marginalized, foreign capital participation under joint venture arrangements was very limited. The slow opening to FDI over the period 1968–1985 had, by the mid-1980s, resulted in limited inflows. The cumulative stock of foreign capital that had been invested at that time in the Central and East European economies was less than USD 250 million.

Inflow of foreign investments to the countries of the region began to gain momentum in the late 1980s. In response to their opening up, after 1988, inflows increased dramatically in terms of both average number of investments and their values, most notably in Hungary and Poland, as a recognition of their pioneer role in the region. At the beginning of 1990 accumulated foreign investment reached USD 250 million in Hungary, and USD 110 million in Poland. In 1990 the value of invested foreign capital in the Central and East European economies grew by more than 100%. Then the inflow of FDI accelerated, as there was a threefold increase in 1991. During the following two years the value of invested foreign capital had again doubled yearly, but in 1994 there was a substantial decrease in foreign capital inflow into the Central and East European economies.

Within the region, the most outstanding results have been achieved by Hungary where the cumulative stock of FDI – in consequence of massive inflows of USD 411 million in 1990, USD 1459 million in 1991, USD 1471 million in 1992 – exceeded USD 3.5 billion by the end of 1992. This meant that more than half of the foreign investments in the East-Central European countries was invested in Hungary. In the first half of 1993 there was an inflow of USD 651 million and the second half of the year brought even more impressive results; thus, there was a total foreign capital inflow of USD 2.3 billion in Hungary in 1993. The next year, 1994, produced poorer results, since the net inflow of FDI amounted to USD 1097 million. The cumulative stock of FDI at the end of 1994 exceeded USD 6.94 billion, still representing the biggest share in foreign investments in the region.

Foreign investment has also increased significantly in Poland. Following the enactment of the New Foreign Investment Law at the beginning of 1989, a total of 4350 foreign investment projects had been authorized by 15 June, 1991. In the whole year of 1991, the net inflow of foreign capital amounted to USD 300 million, so by the end of that year the cumulative stock of FDI in Poland reached USD 509 million (it was USD 112 million in 1989). From 1992, Poland has attracted greater attention from foreign investors. The inflow of FDI accelerated even more: it amounted to USD 665 million in 1992 and to almost USD 1.7 billion in 1993. Thus the cumulative stock of FDI reached USD 1.2 billion at the end of 1992 and, according to the Polish State Agency for Foreign Investment, foreign companies had invested more than USD 2.88 billion by the end of 1993. The remarkable increase of 1993 did not continue in the following year, which produced worse results. In January–October 1994 the net inflow of FDI amounted to only USD 527 million.

In the first years of the transformation, the inflow of foreign investment was relatively low in the Czech Republic and Slovakia compared to the other East-Central European countries. In 1989, there was a meagre inflow of USD 15 million foreign capital into the former Czechoslovakia. After 1989 a considerable increase took place with the inflow of USD 186 million in 1990 and USD 592 million in 1991, but the breakthrough was achieved in 1992 when the inflow of foreign capital amounted to more than USD 1.05 billion. As a result of this great increase, the cumulative stock of FDI in the former Czechoslovakia reached USD 2.15 billion by the end of 1992. It is worth mentioning that almost 90% of this amount fell on Bohemia. This privileged status of Czech territories can be traced back to various reasons. On the one hand, Prague was the capital of the federal state, so the government offices and agencies dealing with foreign investors were located there. On the other hand, Bohemia's geographical and geopolitical position was much more favourable (Germany's neighbourhood, closeness to other West European countries). Last, but not least, there were serious political considerations as well (the Czech political stability and commitment to economic transformation were much more persuasive than Slovakia's ambiguous course).

This tendency has prevailed also after the dissolution of the Czechoslovak state. Foreign investors have paid much more attention to the new Czech Republic than to its Slovak counterpart. By the end of 1993 the cumulative stock of FDI reached USD 2.52 billion in the Czech Republic. In 1994 the net inflow of foreign capital amounted to USD 779 million, thus the cumulative stock of FDI was more than USD 3.3 billion. In Slovakia, in the first half of 1993 the inflow of foreign capital amounted to only USD 90 million and the second half produced even more disappointing results. Thus, its total capital inflow was only USD 120 million. According to the Central Statistical Office of the new Slovak Republic, up to the end of 1993, foreign companies invested USD 326 million in Slovakia. In 1994 basically the same result was achieved. The inflow of FDI amounted to USD 108 million, thus the stock of FDI reached USD 434 million.

Sectoral distribution

As regards the sectoral distribution of FDI in the "Visegrád countries" (the Czech Republic, Hungary, Poland and Slovakia), it can be stated that foreign companies (joint ventures and wholly foreign-owned companies as well) have concentrated their activity almost exclusively on manufacturing and services. In all countries, manufacturing has been the most important sector for the invested capital.

In Hungary, until mid-1993, some 65–67% of a total of about USD 5.3 billion foreign capital had been invested in manufacturing. In 1991 foreign investors took the greatest interest in machinery. This branch accounted for more than 20% of the total capital contribution. (It is worth mentioning that non-electrical machinery was the most important branch with 14% of the ventures, in terms of numbers, while its share in capitalization was much lower, only 6%. Electrical engineering, in contrast, attracted 5% of the ventures, but accounted for more than 14% of the invested capital.) In 1992 food-processing was the most preferred sector, followed by chemical industries. Besides the above-mentioned branches, foreign investors showed considerable interest in the textile, clothing and leather industries. There has been a very impressive development in the car industry. The list of the largest investments was headed by General Motors and the second place was occupied by Suzuki.

In the service sector, foreign investors preferred business services, rental and leasing of machinery, computer-related services, banking and insurance. Foreign companies showed particular interest in trade, including not only foreign trade but internal wholesale and retail trade as well. In terms of the number of ventures, the service sector was the first. However, regarding capitalization, it lagged considerably behind manufacturing until 1993, when the percentage of so-called non-material services rose steeply from 12% to 40% compared to the previous year.

In Poland, foreign companies invested mainly in manufacturing and services. At the end of 1993, manufacturing accounted for 67.5% in terms of invested capital. Within manufacturing, foreign investors preferred food-processing and engineering. During 1993, the food-processing industry registered quite a few large-scale foreign direct investments (Kraft–Jacobs–Suchard, Nestlé, Unilever, Bahlsen, etc.). At the end of 1993, in terms of capitalization, food-processing and engineering (including transport equipment) accounted for 19.5% each, followed by the building industry (17.8%) and chemical industry (13.6%). In services, foreign investors took particular interest in foreign trade, banking and insurance. The share of financial services in capitalization accounted for 13.6%.

Up to the end of 1992 foreign direct investments in the former Czechoslovakia were also concentrated on manufacturing. Within manufacturing, foreign investors preferred the automobile industry, but in terms of capitalization, the chemical industry and food-processing also took a considerable share. In consequence of the Philip Morris deal, the percentage of foreign capital became highest in the tobacco industry. With regard to foreign direct investments implemented until October 1993, the tobacco industry accounted for 26.3% in terms of invested capital. It was followed by the automobile industry with its 21.3%. The third branch was food-processing with 9.6%.

In the service sector, foreign investors took the strongest position in financial services. The share of financial services in the invested capital was more than 9%. In contrast to Poland and Hungary, the percentage of trade was rather low. Regarding capitalization, the share of trade was less than 5%.

Foreign direct investments in Slovakia were also concentrated on manufacturing. In terms of capitalization, more than half of the investments fell on manufacturing. Within manufacturing, machinery, food-processing and chemical industries took the biggest share. It must be emphasized that trade – in contrast to the Czech Republic – in terms of the invested capital accounted for almost 23%. Besides trade, financial and business-related services also took a considerable share. Financial services accounted for 8.7%, the share of business-related services was 5.6%.

Regional distribution

The geographical location of FDI in the East-Central European countries has shown many similarities. In all countries concerned, the regional distribution of foreign companies can be characterized by serious disparities. Foreign investors' decisions concerning investment locations were strongly influenced by considerations of transport and communication possibilities. The reason for this was the regrettable fact that the physical infrastructure has been undeniably poor in all countries concerned. As a consequence, foreign investors have given priority to those parts of the East-Central European countries that were closer to their homeland, to the heart of Europe. The traditionally more developed western parts of the Visegrád countries have proved much more successful in attracting foreign companies. Another major characteristic of regional distribution has been the marked concentration of foreign companies in the capitals of these countries. Thus foreign direct investments have markedly contributed to the increasing regional disparity in all countries concerned.

In Hungary, almost two thirds of the foreign companies, both in terms of numbers and capitalization, were located in Budapest or in its neighbourhood at the end of 1991. By the end of 1993, the share of Budapest and its surrounding had decreased to a certain extent, but it still had the biggest share in FDI, by locating approximately half of the foreign capital invested in Hungary. Furthermore, it can be stated in general that in the western part of the country, much more foreign companies can be found than in the less developed eastern and southern parts. (As a matter of fact, up to 1991 southern Hungary was successful in attracting foreign investors, but the escalation of the civil war in Yugoslavia disastrously hit that part of Hungary – and not only in this respect.)

The unambiguous regional disparity of FDI can be clearly seen if the data of different counties of Hungary are compared. At the end of 1993, in terms of FDI per capita, figures of Győr-Sopron-Moson, Vas and Zala counties were 9–10 times higher than those of Szabolcs-Szatmár-Bereg and Békés.

In the case of Poland, similar tendencies can be identified. Nevertheless, the regional disparity of foreign investments is not so marked here as in Hungary. It is a clear sign of less pronounced concentration that the role of Warsaw and its region – compared with Budapest – is considerably smaller. At the end of 1991, Warsaw and its region, in terms of number of ventures, accounted for 32%, in terms of the invested capital its share was 30%. In this respect, the situation has remained stable. In mid-1993, Warsaw and its region, both in terms of numbers and capitalization, accounted for 33% of the FDI invested in Poland. Besides Warsaw, the two major harbours, Gdansk and Szczecin, furthermore Poznan in western Poland and Katowice, the centre of Upper Silesia, achieved remarkable results in attracting foreign companies. These five regions took almost three fifths of the foreign capital invested in Poland. Wroclaw, Lódz and Krakow also managed to attract sizeable amounts of FDI. In contrast to the above-mentioned territories, the eastern and southeastern parts of Poland produced rather disappointing results in this field. However, in spite of poor records of its eastern and southeastern parts, Poland has the least distorted regional distribution of FDI.

The geographical location of foreign capital invested in the Czech Republic can also be characterized by considerable regional differences. Foreign investors have concentrated their activity on Prague and Central Bohemia. In October 1993, in terms of capitalization, Prague accounted for 28.2% of the foreign capital invested in the Czech Republic, Central Bohemia's share was 33.5%. Apart from Prague and Central Bohemia, the northern part of the country achieved remarkable results by attracting 14% of foreign capital. Western Bohemia and Northern Moravia have been badly hit by structural crises, so their records were rather poor. In consequence of the so far relatively limited Austrian interest, the southern part of the country lagged considerably behind the central and northern territories, despite its generally favourable conditions. The importance of the geographical factor has been convincingly shown by the example of Eastern Bohemia which, like the southern part in general, offers favourable conditions, but attracted only 1.3% of the foreign capital invested in the Czech Republic.

The most serious disparity in the regional distribution of foreign direct investments can be found in the new Slovak Republic. In mid-1993, as a clear sign of the most pronounced concentration in terms of capitalization, Bratislava and its region accounted for more than 70% of the foreign investments. Bratislava's share in FDI was 56%. Besides Bratislava and its region, sizeable amounts of foreign capital have been invested in Poprad. The cumulative share of the above-mentioned territories in FDI reached 85%.

Major investors

In capital exports directed to the countries of the Visegrád group, four countries are of predominant importance: Germany, the United States, Austria and France. With regard to the amount of invested capital till the end of 1993, Germany took the first place, as 28% of FDI was received from there, 22% came from the United States, 11% originated from Austria. France was involved by 8%, the share of the United Kingdom and Italy accounted for 4% each.

There are significant differences between the leading capital exporters in their investing activity in the East-Central European countries. In terms of preferred business location, American investments have been concentrated on Hungary and to a lesser extent on Poland. Germany has achieved the highest percentage in the Czech Republic. Both countries have obtained a leading role in investment activities in all countries of the region. The Austrians have preferred Hungary and Slovakia in choosing investment locations.

Differences between German, American, Austrian and French direct investments can be identified not only in their geographical preferences, but also in terms of preferred activities. German and Austrian investors put the greatest stress on machinery and transport equipment and food-processing; the French preferred chemical industry, food-processing and services. The Americans took the widest range, they paid special attention to the energy sector, food-processing, electrical machinery and transport equipment.

Besides the differences in sectoral and geographical distribution, the German, American, Austrian and French investments differ considerably in terms of average statutory capital of operational enterprises. American and French investments have been implemented overwhelmingly by large companies. In contrast, among the German and Austrian investments there have been a great number of small and medium-sized companies registered. The average statutory capital of French operational enterprises exceeded 2.5 times that of the German and Austrian ones. American investments were of an even bigger size, however, the effect of American and French companies on the host East-Central European economies has been much more limited than their German (and Austrian) counterparts. This phenomenon was due to the much smaller number of American and French investments in East-Central Europe.

It is worth mentioning that there was a conspicuous absence of Japan as foreign investor in the region, especially in view of the fact that worldwide this country accounts for the largest outflow of FDI. In the East-Central European region, less than 1% of the foreign capital invested in joint ventures originated from Japanese companies. The overwhelming majority of Japanese investments in the countries of the region was in services, such as sales and after-sale services for Japanese industrial products, and there were only a few in manufacturing. The latter ones were founded almost exclusively in Hungary, which was the main target country for Japan's investments in the region.

In Hungary, the distribution of leading foreign investors has shown considerable fluctuations in recent years. At first foreign investments were dominated by German and Austrian companies. In 1990 more than 60% of the invested foreign capital originated from American companies and the percentage of Germany fell below 20%. In consequence of these developments, at the end of 1991, half of the invested capital was American, and West European investors accounted for about one third of the FDI stock. The remaining part was mainly composed of Far Eastern (predominantly Japanese and South Korean) investors. In 1992 there were dramatic falls in both American and Far Eastern investments, so the share of West Europeans showed a sizeable increase. The percentage of EC (European Community) member-states rose to 46.6% and the share of EFTA (European Free Trade Association) countries increased to 18%. Flows in 1993 were characterized by basically the same proportions. Nevertheless, till the end of 1993, 28–30% of the invested foreign capital was American, almost one fourth originated from Germany, Austria accounted for approximately 10%, the share of French and Italian investors both amounted to 6–7%. Besides the above-mentioned foreigners, the Japanese and South Korean investors, furthermore the Swedish and Finnish companies obtained a sizeable percentage in foreign investments.

At the end of 1993 the list of the largest investors was headed by General Motors (USD 250 million invested, USD 50 million committed). The second place was occupied by Suzuki (USD 225 million invested, USD 25 million committed). It was followed by General Electric (USD 200 million invested, USD 25 million committed) which took over Tungsram, one of Hungary's most successful companies.

In Poland, foreign investment has been relatively concentrated as regards its origin. In 82% of the foreign investment projects authorized by 1 January 1991, the partners were from Western Europe. Of these, 59% came from the EC and 23% from EFTA countries. The shares were similar in terms of capital committed. Western Europe accounted for 80.5% of the total amount, of which EC member-states contributed 54.5% and EFTA countries 26%. Germany was the largest investor, followed by Sweden, the United States, Austria and the United Kingdom.

By the end of 1993 the geographical structure of FDI has considerably changed. The United States has become the leading foreign investor as regards both the number of enterprises and capitalization. The stock of American investment exceeded USD 1 billion and accounted for 36% of the cumulative stock of FDI. The list of the 10 largest foreign investors in Poland included 4 American companies (Coca-Cola, International Paper, Curtis, Procter and Gamble). It is worth mentioning that 35 American companies which have gone to Poland are among the 500 largest companies listed by the *Fortune* magazine.

At the end of 1993 Italy took the second place after the United States among Poland's most important foreign investors. This fact was the result of two large Italian involvements in 1992 carried out by Fiat and Lucchini. Germany fell back to the third place. By number of investments, the Germans retained their first place, because there were quite a number of small and medium-sized undertakings. The biggest German investor, Henkel AG, ranked only 24th on the list of largest foreign investments with its USD 31 million. Germany was followed by France and the Netherlands (their percentage amounted to 8 and 6, respectively). The importance of previous leading investors (namely Sweden, the United Kingdom, and to a lesser extent Austria) has decreased considerably by the end of 1993. (The Swedish and British share fell to 2% each.)

The list of the largest investors was headed by Fiat (USD 180 million invested, USD 1.8 billion committed). The second place was occupied by Coca-Cola (USD 170 million invested, USD 50 million committed). It was followed by International Paper (USD 120 million invested, USD 175 million committed) which took over the largest paper factory in Poland.

In the Czech Republic, foreign direct investments in terms of origin have shown the heaviest concentration within the region. The main reason for this phenomenon has been the massive German presence. Germany's special position was marked by the fact that at the end of 1991 more than half of the FDI stock originated from German companies. Since then the importance of German investors has decreased to a certain extent: at the end of 1992 the share of German companies in the invested foreign capital accounted for 37.4%, and by the end of 1993 it declined to 31.3%. American investments have taken the opposite direction. In 1992 the United States overtook Germany in terms of annual capital inflow. At the end of 1992 American companies accounted for 21.5% of the invested foreign capital and by the end of 1993 their share rose to 29%. The third place after Germany and the United States was occupied by French investors, accounting for 13.1% of FDI stock. They were followed by Belgian companies representing 7.4% of capitalization. It is worth mentioning that the Austrians have shown rather limited interest in investing in the Czech Republic. In 1993, however, as a result of considerably increased inflow, Austria's share in the cumulative stock of FDI rose from 4.8% to 5.5%.

In the Slovak Republic, the most important foreign investor has been Austria in terms of both the number of ventures and capitalization. Until October 1993, 29% of the invested foreign capital came from Austria. The second place was occupied by Germany, representing more than 18% of capitalization. Besides Austria and Germany, the United States and France also have a considerable share in foreign investments. The United States accounted for 15% of the cumulative stock of FDI, French investors represented 10%.

The regulatory framework of foreign direct investments

Under earlier legislation, foreign enterprises were often excluded from certain areas (for example, in banking and financial services), from engaging in foreign trade and from fully owning their business. In addition, they were often obliged to invest a minimum sum in the foundation capital of a foreign affiliate.

In the wake of the political and economic transition in the East-Central European countries, the legislation of FDI has been reconsidered. All countries have tried to create more attractive conditions for FDI by amending their existing laws and regulations or by promulgating new legislation. Although laws and regulations in the countries concerned differ from various aspects, there are a number of common elements aiming largely at separating public administration from actual economic management. Screening procedures have been simplified and the scope and eligibility for partnerships expanded. Principles concerning the repatriation of profits, foreign majority shareholdings and taxation have been substantially modified and a number of important legal guarantees against expropriations and divestment have been provided to foreign companies.

According to acts on foreign investments in the East-Central European countries, a foreign investor is to be compensated at real value and without delay for the losses incurring from any nationalization, expropriation or other measure having an equivalent effect on the foreign investor's property. The compensation is to be paid to the foreign investor in the currency of investment.

All East-Central European countries have now valid investment-protection agreements with almost every significant partner-country from which direct investment is received. At the end of the 1980s and at the beginning of the 1990s all countries concerned joined the convention on the Settlement of Investment Disputes Between States and Nationals of Other States.

National treatment and most-favoured-nation treatment constitute an important part of the investment protection agreements concluded by the East-Central European countries. However, the agreements allow for some exemptions from the most-favoured-nation treatment.

In financial terms, foreign investors in all East-Central European countries are allowed to repatriate their profits earned in both local and foreign currencies, as well as their original capital investment. However, before the introduction of internal convertibility

112

– especially in Poland, but to a lesser extent in the former Czechoslovakia as well – foreign investors were restricted in the amount they could repatriate, and were often forced to use a complicated system of barter in order to extract the profit from their activities. It must be emphasized that since mid-1991 foreign investors do not need any licence to transfer all their after-tax profits abroad, as well as their proceeds from selling shares. Also, profits and proceeds from liquidation of assets can be repatriated without permission.

As regards the right of establishment and equity rules, legislation in the East-Central European countries has moved towards granting foreign legal entities the same right of establishment as domestic enterprises have. In some instances, notably in Hungary, foreign investors have acquired rights superior to domestic companies. On the other hand, the legislation in some cases still allows governments to exclude foreign investors from particular industries. Generally, for joint ventures in the banking sector, the authorization of the central banks continues to be required.

In Hungary, there are no equity and sectoral limitations, and the establishment of corporate associations with foreign participation is possible without special governmental approval. In other words, the Hungarian authorities have imposed the automatic approval system.

In Poland, there is no equity limitation, it is possible to establish wholly foreign-owned companies as well, and approval procedures have been shortened and simplified. But in certain – mainly defence-related – fields, a feasibility study is required for obtaining permission.

In the Czech and the Slovak Republics, government approval must be obtained for joint ventures with state enterprises. Approval is required from the Ministry of Finance. A decision must be made within 60 days after submission of the application. Defence- and security-related sectors are excluded for foreign investors.

In connection with liability of foreign investment for taxation and tax allowances, it can be stated that foreign investors pay taxes in the countries of East-Central Europe, but initially the rates were much lower than for domestic companies. Nevertheless, the easing of restrictions on profit repatriation has generally led to a less favourable fiscal treatment for foreign investors. For example, in its Foreign Investment Law of 14 June 1991, Poland reduced its tax rates and abolished its automatic three-year tax holiday for new foreign investment projects. Since then, fiscal incentives have been awarded only if the project boosts employment or exports, is in a priority industry, or is located in a designated area. The same happened in Hungary where the amendment of Act XXIV of 1988 on Foreign Investment in 1990 reduced tax rates considerably and shortened the term of tax holidays. Generally, in all countries of East-Central Europe, tax-related and other fiscal incentives have been awarded more selectively in the latest years.

The countries of East-Central Europe rely exclusively on fiscal incentives to attract foreign direct investments. It has been a general phenomenon that authorities in East-Central Europe have given priority to attracting investments in large-scale manufacturing. This preference has led to a tendency to consider investments made by small and medium-sized foreign companies, especially in services, as less favourable even though both small and medium-sized enterprises and the service sector are underdeveloped in the whole area.

According to national regulations, large foreign investors may apply for corporate profit tax relief on terms similar to small and medium-sized companies. However, this concept has worked in theory only. The real practice has shown quite a different development. Large foreign investors (for example General Electric and Suzuki in Hungary, Fiat in Poland, Volkswagen and Philip Morris in Bohemia) have proved very successful in obtaining additional preferences from the governments. This fact, however, undermined considerably the declared normativity and reliability of the national regulations in the region.

Motives for investing in the region

The collapse of the communist regimes and the withdrawal of the Soviet army were prior requirements for an increase in FDI. The member countries of the Visegrád group have achieved clear advantage over the other East European states in transforming their economy and society. The Visegrád countries (with the partial exemption of Slovakia) have been firmly committed to developing market economy and creating parliamentary democracy and a pluralistic society. The upswing of foreign investment activity taking place despite the serious slamp of production and consumption suggests that the main stimulus for investing in the region has been the progress of systemic transformation and political stability.

The Visegrád countries have achieved remarkable progress in establishing legal frameworks comparable to those in Western Europe for regulating FDI (including repatriation guarantees, investment protection, and agreements to avoid double taxation). Moreover, they allow 100% foreign ownership and offer special tax concessions to foreign investors. These developments have considerably reduced the so-called country-specific risks, since an established legal framework is of predominant importance for business calculations. A substantial liberalization of foreign trade and of domestic price formation, furthermore, the introduction of some kind of internal currency convertibility also had favourable effects on investment decisions.

There is a unique opportunity for Western corporations in the Visegrád countries, as this is the time for these countries to initiate the privatization of their state-owned companies, providing Western corporations with the possibility of acquiring companies in the region for a relatively good price.

For foreign investors, the aim of investing in the region is to acquire new markets, to take over markets already covered by former state-owned companies. Having analysed available information on existing cases of foreign investment, it has turned out that in the overwhelming majority of cases, the foreign investors' motivation was to get hold of the domestic market as well as the foreign market of the given East-Central European companies.

On the other hand, investors also want to expand production at low production cost. In this respect the price of labour, real estate and energy are taken into consideration, as well as the level of environmental protection, furthermore, tax holidays and other benefits provided for foreign investors. The price of labour, real estate and energy in the Visegrád countries are much lower than in Western Europe, not to speak of the much less tight environmental regulation. Foreign investors almost unanimously agree that the labour force in the region is talented, relatively appropriately skilled, creative and disciplined. In addition, it is quite cheap by international standards. However, taking into account labour cost per produced unit, the relative labour cost advantage may shrink considerably, due to the relatively low level of productivity in the Visegrád countries. Nevertheless, production cost has so far not been the dominant driving force of foreign involvement, as it has been convincingly shown in the case of Hungary and Slovakia. In spite of having the highest production costs in the region, Hungary has proved quite successful in attracting FDI, while Slovakia, the region's cheapest country, has produced rather poor results in this field.

The geographical location of the Visegrád countries is a further attraction to FDI. Poland and the Czech Republic have been EU (European Union) neighbours and with Austria's joining, Hungary and Slovakia have also become EU neighbours. The possibility of their ultimate membership and the consequent market access is another factor for non-EU investing countries, like the United States and Japan. At the same time, the Visegrád countries have close contacts with other East and Central European markets, including Russia and Ukraine, where direct involvement is considered too risky. Under these circumstances, exporting from the Visegrád countries is regarded as a workable solution to this problem. It cannot be denied that cost and proximity together play an important role in investment decisions. Mainly for German and Austrian companies, a nearby production site in bordering countries provides an easily feasible alternative to expensive domestic production.

Barriers to foreign investment

The unsettled conditions of the post-socialist transition in the East-Central European countries have, however, created serious difficulties in attracting the desired FDI inflows. The investment climate in the region is rather complex. The common problem areas are as follows:

Legal and regulatory conditions. Policy-makers have had to work out a new legal framework under rapidly changing circumstances and their inexperience in the regulation of FDI have many times resulted in a typically ad hoc, piecemeal approach. The regulation of FDI in the East-Central European countries is quite liberal in international comparison and this fact improves the region's chance for attracting foreign investors. However, the competitive advantage of liberal regulation has been largely eroded because of the instability of the legal conditions for foreign investment.

Economic conditions. All East-Central European countries are passing through a severe economic crisis, reflected in sharp decline in industrial output, the collapse of traditional export markets, unprecedented unemployment and strong inflationary pressures. Pending restructuring, the underdeveloped areas of the economy, the undeniably poor shape of the physical infrastructure – especially in telecommunications – impede the FDI process. In the case of Hungary and to a lesser extent of Poland, a heavy burden of external debt had added to the traditional scarcity of hard currencies.

Political conditions. From a monolithic, one-party rule, the East-Central European countries have shifted to fractured, multi-party politics. In all countries concerned, governments are struggling with daunting economic and social problems. The collapse of the communist rule has led to the eruption of previously oppressed tensions in both external and internal relations. To ease the symptoms of severe economic crisis, governments in the East-Central European countries have become more and more indulgent to protectionist pressures in intra-regional trade. The growing tendency towards protectionism may deter a considerable part of the existing and potential investors from the region, who originally intended to found their activity on exports to other East-Central European countries.

Institutional conditions. The transformation of the East-Central European societies involves sweeping changes. However, the processes of marketization, privatization and reintegration into the world economy will inevitably be long and difficult. Meanwhile, the institutional legacies of the centrally planned system create obstacles to FDI. Due to bureaucratic inefficiency, it quite frequently takes an intolerably long time to obtain the necessary documents. The inadequately functioning financial sector is one of the most serious bottlenecks in the transformation process. Banking services are of very poor quality. Moreover, low quality is coupled with high prices, thus practically all major investor countries have their corresponding banks in the East-Central European countries, offering services superior to those of the domestic financial institutions. Deficient flow of information causes many problems as well. Information on sales of state-owned companies is hardly available, there is a chronic shortage of foreign language pamphlets with general information about the East-Central European countries.

Prospects of foreign investments in the countries of the Visegrád group

Statistical data of recent years have convincingly shown that the barriers to FDI have weighed less than the advantages when investment decisions have been made. Hungary, Poland and the Czech Republic, as a result of two or three years of massive capital inflow, have gradually attained the so-called threshold level at which it becomes necessary for less interested investors to invest in these countries. Slovakia faces gloomier prospects in consequence of its political instability and ambiguous economic policy.

It is a fact that the number and statutory capital of joint ventures have soared up since 1988, although the actual inflow of foreign capital compared to other regions of the world (the Unites States, the EC, Southeast Asia) has remained rather modest. Starting from a very low base, the growth of FDI has appeared very impressive, yet is often to be attributed to individual large-scale projects.

In terms of invested foreign capital, a more balanced distribution can be envisaged in the region, since flow data for 1994 clearly show Poland and the Czech Republic catching up rapidly, so Hungary's privileged position has been fading.

Finally, it may be questioned whether the expansion of foreign capital inflow is a temporary phenomenon or not. Hungary's example suggests that the big increase of foreign investment might be a temporary phenomenon, and after a few years the amount of foreign capital inflow may stabilize. However, it might be premature to generalize this example.

Bibliography

Butterworths Journal of International Banking and Financial Law, London, 1992.

East–West Investment and Joint Ventures News. United Nations Economic Commission for Europe, Geneva, 1989–1993.

Economic Survey of Europe in 1993–1994. UN Economic Commission for Europe, Geneva, 1994.

Economic Survey of Europe in 1994–1995. UN Economic Commission for Europe, Geneva, 1995.

Fact File, National Agency of Foreign Investment, Bratislava, 1993.

Mádi, I. (1993): *Foreign Direct Investment in Hungary.* Institute for World Economics of the Hungarian Academy of Sciences, Budapest.

Poland: International Economic Report 1992/93. IWE, Warsaw.

Samuelsson, H.-F. (1992): *Foreign Direct Investments in Eastern Europe: Current Situation and Potential.* Geneva.

Schnabel, C. (1993): *Die Arbeitsbeziehungen im Osteuropäischen Transformationsprozess.* Universität Köln.

The Czech Republic, More than Prague. Bank Austria Wien, 1993.

World Investment Directory 1992. World Bank, Washington, 1993.

World Investment Directory 1993. World Bank, Washington, 1994.

Ownership change and performance in companies of the former socialist countries of Europe

MIKLÓS SZANYI

Most of the transforming economies of East-Central Europe finished their fifth year after much political and economic turmoil. Five years' time seems long enough to assess how far the companies of these countries have moved away from their paternalistic past toward a market economic future. Were they able and willing to adjust themselves to the challenges of this new environment? Were the governments able to support corporate adjustment and modernization? To what degree have the microeconomic frames of the market economic system been instituted in these countries?

Microeconomic changes provide the backbone of economic restructuring and modernization. The establishment of economic and political stability in the transforming countries necessitates the evolution of companies and of microeconomic conditions in a market-conform manner. The speed and depth (but also, probably the future) of the transformation process depend on this.

Challenges to be coped with

Some of the basic changes of the economic environment, many of which are well described elsewhere,[1] should be recalled. These changes and challenges may be divided into two groups: systemic changes (internal to companies), and working condition changes (external to companies).[2] Both groups contain elements fundamental to the sustainability of the operations of companies.

---

[1] For example in Lipton and Sachs (1990); for Russia see: Rostowski (1993); for Poland see: Rapacki (1991); for Hungary see: Szanyi (1992).

[2] The most important elements of the systemic change are: the change of the ownership structure; the establishment of effective corporate governance structures; the change in the applied managerial practices (a shift from the execution of commands to independent and responsible decision-making); the establishment of an up-to-date information and communication system within the company, together with the introduction of a new, more suitable corporate institutional buildup.

Changes in the external conditions were rather well known. Some of the most important ones were the collapse of the CMEA (Council of Mutual Economic Assistance) and the eastern markets, decline in public procurement and sluggish domestic demand on the demand side. On the supply side, competition was increased through various liberalization steps and through the cessation of governmental subsidies. Also an important change was the severe credit crunch set on the companies in several transforming economies as part of an overall tightening of the monetary policies applied.

The group of socialist countries formed a separate world. The elimination of this separation caused all kinds of shocking effects. Companies were more or less directly exposed to these effects. In most cases, governments lacked the financial means, and many times also the political willingness, to maintain the same degree of prior protection. The collapse of the regional economic co-operation and the resolute break with the old-fashioned ties in the forerunner countries of economic and political reforms, limited the room for manoeuvrability in the less enthusiastic countries as well. Thus, the first serious change came from the external markets.

The drop in Eastern sales very strongly affected the companies of the transforming economies. Five to twenty per cent of the individual countries' total GDP was sold on regional markets.[3] In the case of more open (small) countries, the market loss was bigger, especially if the former economic regime discouraged the development of economic links with advanced market economies. In addition, recession had just started concurrently in the West European and American markets, causing a severe drop in world trade and a remarkable spread of protectionist measures.

Sales opportunities contracted severely on the domestic markets as well: first, because of the declining demand (including public procurement in many cases); and second, because of the unprecedentedly quick opening of the markets for foreign competition. Domestic companies could hardly stand foreign competition. Their production was inferior in terms of performance, quality and reliability. After-sales services were almost unknown and companies were also seriously undercapitalized. This made any serious effort to improve production and sales almost impossible.

Interestingly enough, many companies tried to find a way out of the sales crisis through a rapid increase of Western export sales. The introduction of the General System of Preferences in the trade of most transforming economies improved the companies' competitiveness. Western exports could, however, not replace much of the losses in the domestic and Eastern markets. More importantly, they could not compensate for the serious financial losses which occurred when commercial banks drastically increased the interest charged on earlier loans.

In order to successfully cope with the external challenges, companies have to adjust themselves to the new requirements. Ideally, the restructuring of companies should occur simultaneously in several domains. First and most important is the streamlining of activities: useless assets should be sold; unviable activities given up; and hidden unemployment drastically reduced. All this means the immediate cut of loss-making activities.[4]

Then the system of corporate governance and management should be changed. Perhaps it would be easier first to restructure the system of corporate management and decision-making. This could be supported relatively cheaply with the establishment of an up-to-date information system in the companies. Modern information equipment would allow managers to be introduced to the latest and more effective management practices.

But increased and effective managerial activity for the sake of corporate adjustment can only be expected under effective corporate governance structures. The ownership

---

[3] The size of the losses that occurred e.g. in Hungary can be best illustrated by the example of Austria. Namely, CMEA sales played a role in Hungary equal to Austria's sales to Germany.

[4] Grosfeld and Roland (1995) refer to this activity as defensive restructuring. Strategic restructuring means, in their approach, long-term changes in production, product and sales patterns.

status of the state-owned companies has to be settled as soon as possible. Management is not willing to make any important, strategic decisions for adjustment in an uncertain environment where managers can be fired at any time without explanation and where no clear requirements are set for them.

Privatization seems therefore to be a crucial element of transformation. Without privatization, corporate management does not feel encouraged to stop trying the old, paternalistic solutions, nor to stop bargaining with authorities to soften the budget constraints. The lack of hard budget constraints inevitably blocks adjustment processes and the search for increasing effectiveness.

Once the conditions of the market-conform activity of the companies are established, the companies immediately face technological challenges. The long technological isolation of the observed countries produced very marked technological backwardness, which has to be eliminated if companies intend to regain competitive strength.

It is difficult to imagine that companies, which have just suffered such severe losses and damages, would be able to finance investments of a magnitude that facilitates the introduction of up-to-date products and production.[5] The role of foreign capital as well as state support seem to be necessary here. It is crucial, however, not to pour much capital aimed at technological modernization into companies of an uncertain ownership status.

The special role of the governments in assisting corporate transformation should also be emphasized. With the creation of the market economic frames on the one hand, governmental decisions may trigger shocking effects on companies. On the other hand, political struggles as well as the transformation of political power into an economic one, urge authorities to get deeply involved in microeconomic decision-making. This latter activity is often bound to the softening of the just crunched budget constraints. Political and economic philosophy and actual policy-making are frequently confronted. Thus, the applied economic policy often undergoes significant changes. The highly politicized microeconomic transformation process prevents governments from applying steady and coherent microeconomic policies.

On the other hand, it is rather obvious that the microeconomic transformation process needs state assistance. Privatization, reorganization and recapitalization of companies can only be carried out with active state involvement. Also, many sizeable companies need state intervention at least in order to facilitate a smooth market exit and not to allow an immediate collapse.[6] A more civilized solution of state intervention may be the establishment of a rather small group of state companies willing to remain for a longer term under state control. If intervention is unavoidable, governments should try at least to set the limits to direct intervention and not to remain directly exposed to the pressure of any company.

Governments of the transforming economies may intervene in favour of state-owned companies with a tolerable level of moral hazard. First of all, the government should use indirect means of sales support, such as the establishment and improvement of trade development agencies and financial institutions. Such institutions are important especially in the case of Eastern markets. Another option is the development of specific management contracts with private vendors to restructure and improve state companies.

[5] In the sense of Grosfeld's and Roland's (1995) strategic restructuring.

[6] State support for ailing branches and for crisis-ridden regions is rather common also in developed market economies. The problem is, however, that the transitional economies' financial resources are rather scarce and should be used for the strengthening of market economic institutions, rather than for undermining them.

Economic policy and corporate transformation

If the East-Central European democracies really think that the good fortune of their nations is bound to the establishment of a fully fledged market economy, then the basic microeconomic task of the governments' economic policies should be the creation and strengthening of market economic frames. This means the abolishment of many market distorting measures and the promotion of competition in the markets, including denationalization and the general reduction of direct state intervention.

The shift from the old paternalistic system is not so easy for corporate managers. It is especially difficult when the state administration is not ready to renounce the old rules, because state bureaucrats are interested in just the opposite.[7] The shift can be facilitated by the careful introduction of measures that drive managers toward the necessary adjustment steps.

The most important measures are to break the market distorting effects and strengthen competition in the domestic markets. They are: subsidy cuts, price and wage liberalization, the breakup of monopolies, trade liberalization (both exports and imports), the liberalization of economic activities and, for certain, the creation of basic economic legislation.[8]

Another set of measures should facilitate the entry to and exit from the market. A new market- (or EU- or GATT-) conform business promotion system has to be established and the institution of bankruptcy needs to be introduced. After privatization, the second most important measure in the creation of the market institutions is bankruptcy. From the financial side, bankruptcy forces payment discipline and efficient activity from companies and corporate managers. Thus, its effect strengthens that of privatization and the establishment of a sound corporate governance structure. Without having any deterrent, even privately founded and foreign-owned companies utilize the same opportunities of soft budget constraints and, for example, build up payment arrears.

Many governments are afraid of the introduction of bankruptcy. They realize that lacking payment discipline as well as unlimited loss-making activity result in a situation where many companies face serious liquidity problems. Governments fear an avalanche of bankruptcies once it is institutionalized.

Bankruptcy in itself is a necessary part of the market economy. Its functions are twofold. First, it enables the smooth exit of companies; second, it provides a necessary deterrent for companies and forces profitable and efficient activities. Both functions are essential in the process of transformation. These functions are the most important tools of strengthening the budget constraints.[9]

It should also be considered that bankruptcy does not necessarily mean the liquidation of a company. The fine details of the bankruptcy regulation may give a fair chance for bankruptcy agreements and reorganizations. But those companies which are not able to prepare a viable reorganization or business plan have probably no chance of survival in the long run, unless the state continues their heavy subsidizing. The exit of such companies is most desirable and their bankruptcy would not necessarily trigger an avalanche of bankruptcies.

---

[7] This is a very widespread phenomenon, but it is felt especially strongly in Romania and Russia.
[8] See e.g. Lipton and Sachs (1990).
[9] For a discussion of this, see: Mizsei (1993).

In order to avoid the sudden deterioration of corporate finances, economic policy should consider the gradual but parallel introduction of the most important liberalization measures (the drive of increasing competition) and the institution of bankruptcy. It is essential to note that companies and managers try to avoid these painful but often necessary adjustment steps. Thus, if there are loopholes in the regulation, i.e. the introduction of certain elements of the system is unfinished, companies will use these loopholes to avoid real adjustment. Payment arrears, hidden unemployment, intense lobbying for subsidies are the most frequent symptoms of incomplete regulation.

Therefore, we suggest the immediate and parallel introduction of the most important liberalization measures together with the institution of bankruptcy, so that the rules of the game be obvious from the very beginning. But the crunch on the companies should be tightened only step by step, avoiding the sudden deterioration of corporate finances. Companies have to be allowed the necessary time for restructuring and adjustment, but no major loopholes should remain in the regulation. For the sake of easier reference, we shall refer to this type of microeconomic policy as "global gradual" policy. This optimal microeconomic policy has not been pursued in any of the transforming economies.

Differences in initial conditions

The success of or the degree to which the global gradual microeconomic policy can be applied depends on many factors. Many of the problems the transitional economies have to face are common. Five to six years ago, observers could have said that Slovenian or Hungarian companies' behaviour is much more market conform than, say, the Russian companies'. In a sense this may have been true, but the basic principles of their functioning were more or less the same anyway. Reform-communist countries let their companies be exposed to certain market economic influences. But the degree of this exposure was rather low and market failure was not punished with bankruptcy. The essence of socialist paternalism was an inherent part of the economies, from Slovenia to Russia.

Consequently, the deep crisis hit the companies in very similar ways and the initial responses were also rather similar. This meant increased stockpiling, lobbying for subsidies and accumulation of payment arrears. There was no big difference in corporate responses at the beginning of the transformation process. Managers tried to make use of the old, soft, paternalistic tactics. This happened in those countries as well where managers had had some market economic experiences. They knew something about strategic planning, total quality control or cash flow analysis. But they had never been forced to introduce modern management practices into their everyday life.

However, one should not think that experiences with market economy, up-to-date knowledge and regular and frequent contacts with the West do not make any difference. But without serious forces, this knowledge and experience will not be mobilized. Also, the relatively independent decision-making of companies in certain countries had contributed to the managerial knowledge. Thus, we may say that Croatia, Hungary, Poland and Slovenia enjoy a clear advantage as far as the extent and quality of the managerial knowledge are concerned.

From a longer historical aspect we may also compare managerial and technical knowledge in Croatia, the Czech Republic, Hungary, Poland, Slovakia and Slovenia. These countries or at least large parts of them have old industrial traditions. The inherited technical but also entrepreneurial culture of these areas may also be important. This is especially clear if we compare different regional development patterns within countries (say, in Poland or in Hungary, or compare the Czech Republic and Slovakia).

Initial conditions were also different in terms of fixed corporate assets. Here again we may refer to historical traditions as far as the structure of the individual national economies is concerned. The remainders of the pre-World War II structures did not disappear entirely, although the so-called "forced socialist industrialization" diverted the economies from their organic development paths.

Nevertheless, there are profound structural changes taking place in some countries under consideration. One line of the changes is directed toward the establishment of a modern economic structure with much less manufacturing and more services. The other direction is shifting back toward those industries and services and agricultural branches that have traditionally gained comparative advantage in the international division of labour.

The intensity of the structural problems faced by the national economies can be traced back to a large extent to the existence of industrial facilities of the "forced socialist industrialization". Another factor that exacerbates the problems is that the region's main trade partners in Western Europe consider the very same industries as sensitive. Thus, no better access to other markets is available even if East-Central European production of steel, aluminium, textiles, cement, etc. is cheaper due to wage differences. Still, there is a comparative advantage in favour of the transforming economies.

Unfortunately, established democracies show little understanding and support for the establishing democracies in the form of market access. Their support often remains on the level of rhetoric and they do not hesitate to apply the toughest protectionist measures immediately when their powerful industrial and agricultural lobbies require so. This is not surprising, and fully understandable. After all, they are also suffering from a long recession. For the first time in modern history, some of them even registered negative economic growth! However, irrespective of this, the establishing market economies have to realize that they cannot rely exclusively on Western support. An extraordinarily strong contraction of the industrial production in the transforming economies seems to be unavoidable.

Basic types of ownership and corporate governance

There was a unanimous understanding among the transforming economies that substantial parts of them should be denationalized. An almost full privatization was foreseen in the former Czechoslovakia, Hungary and Poland. A smaller or larger part of the state-owned companies was to remain in state ownership in other countries (Bulgaria, Romania, Russia). Regardless of the aims of the governments, the actual situation is that a substantial part of the investigated economies cannot be privatized or wound up in liquidation procedures, because they are too important.

Thus, besides the genuine private and privatized sector, there will also be a substantial state sector in all the transforming economies in the long run. Therefore, we may differentiate between companies according to their ownership status. There is the privately founded sector, together with those companies, the privatization of which resulted in direct private ownership. There is another group of formerly state-owned companies:

124

the "quasi privatized" ones. Quasi privatization means commercialization and privatization through ways that do not produce direct private ownership control.[10] And the third group contains the state sector with companies deliberately left in state hands and with those that could not be privatized.

One can clearly see from the above grouping of companies that we make a distinction between privatization methods according to their impact on the ownership structure and on corporate governance. In our view, the basic aim of privatization is the establishment of effective ownership and corporate governance structures. This is an extremely important factor, because it is one of the preconditions of an improvement in corporate activities (corporate adjustment and the increase of efficiency and of competitiveness).[11]

The prehistory of privatization was always considered as one of the most revolutionary innovations of economic policy. It is "a return to principles of individual freedom and private enterprise that have changed the world...".[12] These words describe in a way the profound changes that occurred in the privatized companies, industries and economies. If we take a look at the companies inherited from the socialist regimes, it becomes obvious that without any change, their ownership cannot be based on the traditional classical principles of family ownership. First, because their size and complicated structure prevent owners from exercising direct control over the company (in a classical manner); second, because their privatization usually does not result in a single-person or family ownership form. Only pieces, small items and workshops can be sold to private persons or their associations.

Another widespread ownership form in established market economies is share ownership. Large diversified companies can be privatized more easily when the shares are either distributed or sold (e.g. on the stock exchange). However, one should consider that corporate governance of share-holding companies is executed in indirect ways and, among others, through different mechanisms of the capital and managerial labour markets.[13] These markets are underdeveloped in the post-socialist countries and cannot perform the same functions for corporate governance as those in established market economies.

The methods most commonly used in privatization are direct sale to foreign investors (mainly multinational corporations), transfer to investment funds (mutual funds, privatization investment funds) and preferential sale to numerous small private investors. Privatization through liquidation seems to be the privatization method through which small and medium-sized companies' ownership is established by private persons or their associations. This is especially remarkable in Poland, but is also applied in Hungary. In Russia, venturers also purchased a number of factories and companies through rather dubious deals. Still, the majority of the privatized companies in Eastern and Central Europe does not change the ownership form in a way which facilitates direct control

[10] Owners such as investment funds, property funds and banks which themselves are still state owned cannot be regarded as private. We also count here those companies whose business shares were simply distributed among citizens, since these owners cannot execute any effective control over their companies.

[11] Of course, there are other important aspects of privatization as well. First, political considerations should be mentioned here. Privatization is one of the hottest political issues in most establishing democracies, and political arguments usually do not favour the predominance of the aspects of effective ownership functions. Privatization may also bring revenues to the state budget. Contrary to these aspects, choosing conventional methods may be underpinned with the above argument.

[12] Hanke (1987), p. 18.

[13] For details see: Alchian and Demsetz (1972); Jensen and Meckling (1976); Fama (1980).

of the management. Consequently, it is not an appropriate assumption that the privatized companies' management will necessarily work in a classical manner by maximizing corporate profits.

There are, however, certain factors that determine the likely path of privatization in at least the medium term. These factors affect both the demand and the supply sides of privatization.

On the demand side, economic policy-makers have to take into consideration the different receptivity of the population in these countries. In Poland, but especially in Hungary, there are large groups in the population that had experiences with many of the institutions and practices of a market economy during the last two decades of the socialist regime. Private entrepreneurs started working on their own and corporate managers enjoyed a certain degree of freedom in decision-making. Such experiences were completely suppressed in other countries.

The receptivity of the population influences privatization in different ways. The most obvious is the demand for state properties. Spontaneous and self-privatization in Hungary and privatization through liquidation in Poland were based on the activity of corporate managers and private investors. But market economic experiences positively influence the public opinion toward privatization *per se*. The negative examples of this are the Balkan countries where the fear of social differentiation and political attacks on privatization as a way to rob the peoples' ownership block any kind of privatization.

On the supply side of privatization, the major and ever serious problem is the financial situation of state-owned companies. Supply of these companies may also shrink, because privatization results, which have already been achieved, naturally reduce the scope of the supply. And, of course, it is the better company that gets privatized first (again, regardless of the privatization method applied!). For example, the best couple of hundreds of companies having been sold in Hungary, most companies still on stock at the State Property Agency suffer from serious defects. The scope of the supply is of course further limited by the liquidated companies.

Most of the above-mentioned factors are not favourable in the East-Central European countries. Consequently, privatization cannot be finished overnight. It is important to note here that there is not much difference between those countries that applied distributive methods and those that used competitive methods of privatization. The above factors affect privatization negatively in general. Only the appearance of the problems may be different.

There is a certain convergence of privatization methods in the Visegrád countries (where practical privatization is carried out). Hungary introduced a set of incentives for small domestic investors to encourage their participation. Favourable credit schemes, leasing constructions and the acceptance of the compensation vouchers as means of privatization marked a shift in policy from looking for strategic investors. Stock markets also gain importance in shaping ownership structures in Hungary.

There are also clear signs of a change in the Czech Republic. In the second wave of privatization, less emphasis was placed on the voucher method and two thirds of the offered companies were privatized through conventional methods. Another interesting phenomenon is the revival of the Prague Stock Exchange and the substantial inflow of foreign capital through it. In the trade of business shares not only investment funds take part, but also citizens, and more importantly: foreign investors. This means that we should not consider investment funds any longer as the exclusive long-term owners of Czech companies. More generally, investment funds seem to be interesting and important moderators in voucher privatization, but putting business shares into a handful of (indirectly state-owned) investment funds does not develop long lasting ownership structures.

There is an increasing willingness on part of the funds to effectively influence corporate management, but the realization of the funds' ownership control seems to be extremely difficult. There are some legal barriers in the way of obtaining majority stakes in companies and the co-ordination between funds and other owners is rather difficult. Also, funds are often not able to counterbalance the activity of corporate managers. They have to bargain with corporate leaders as well.

In summary: the privatization process has reached the point where the problem of ownership and corporate governance may be meaningfully discussed only in four countries: the Czech Republic, Hungary, Poland and Slovakia. The mere distribution of vouchers and the establishment of ownership or investment funds with no practical influence on companies in other countries do not seriously challenge the corporate managers' positions and their inherited management practices.

The relationship between ownership structure and performance

There is a rather widespread consensus among economists that one major contributor to the failure of the socialist company was the scattered ownership and control functions of companies and the resulting weaknesses in corporate governance. But the change of the ownership structure of companies occurred under the circumstances of the transition recession, which involved the emergence of major adjustment tasks. The tasks of systemic and business adjustment sometimes contradict each other and thwart quick solutions. They may also go on separately.

Empirical evidence shows that at the early stages of privatization, both Polish and Hungarian companies took certain positive adjustment steps.[14] Many of them were aimed at increasing sales on new markets (i.e. exports). The export boom of the transforming economies may partly be traced back to this phenomenon. There is, however, rather clear evidence that the increase in exports did not facilitate structural changes. Entirely new products were hardly developed. The most important adjustment step aimed at more specialization on Western markets was the introduction of EC standards of production and product quality. Also subcontracting gained much importance.

Modernization of the decision-making system was also typical in many companies. This included mainly the introduction or extension of data and information processing systems and tools of economic analysis that require computer facilities. The efficiency of the systems' utilization remained, however, rather low.

The adjustment steps did not result in the expected turn in corporate performance as far as market share, sales, revenues and profits are concerned. Dabrowski et al. (1992) proved that in the 1990–1992 period, an overall decline in profitability could be registered among the Polish companies, including privatized ones. Hungarian figures showed a drastic decline in capacity utilization during the same period.[15] Thirty per cent of the

---

[14] See: Dabrowski et al. (1990, 1992); Szanyi (1992).
[15] See: Szanyi (1993).

state-owned companies realized a higher than 80% capacity utilization ratio in 1991. In 1992, this number decreased to 15%. The share of bankrupt or nearly bankrupt state-owned companies increased in the same period from 30% to 50%. Labour productivity declined steadily after 1990 also in the Czech Republic.[16]

However, bankruptcy is not an unknown phenomenon in the privately founded or privatized sector either, especially in Hungary. The majority of the bankruptcy filings in Hungary is with small private companies. But neither are large private companies secured in the transition period. Some of the early flagships of the Hungarian private sector went bankrupt in 1993, proving the fact that declining economic performance and the negligence of the limits of company growth may lead to serious imbalances in private companies as well. Thus, declining performance, financial troubles and imbalances are general symptoms of economies under transformation. Weak performances generally characterize the corporate sector and can be regarded as an element of the transformation recession and not necessarily one of systemic change.

It can be drawn as a conclusion that the ownership structure determines corporate performances far less than it was expected.[17] The quality and the ambitions of managers matter much more. The Hungarian experience showed that managers interested in the (potential) ownership of their companies performed much better. There is of course a positive relationship between ownership and performance, but it is also true that the better managers were more able to develop both adjustment strategies for the rescue of the companies and better privatization strategies to secure their position as manager (perhaps also as an owner). Thus, corporate performance and privatization have a link most probably through the manager himself. Hence, privatization and improvement in performance is rather a personal than a systemic question.

There are both positive and negative proofs of this statement. Hungarian and Polish empirical evidence shows that the increase in labour productivity in these countries can be attributed to both private and public (state-owned) companies' performance. Negative examples are found in some Eastern and Southeastern European countries, where the first steps of privatization did not change corporate governance structures. There was not much room left for able managers to take an active part in the legal course of privatization. Consequently, corporate performances continued to decline. Here the complete lack of market economic experiences also had a withholding effect on managers.

Achievements and perspectives

The former socialist block seems to be divided from the point of view of macroeconomic restructuring and adjustment. Privatization steps affecting corporate governance occurred on a mass scale only in the Visegrád countries. These are also the countries where the first signs of microeconomic recovery can be identified. Polish and Hungarian industrial growth and the Czech export performances in 1993 are considered here as the first signs.

---

[16] See: Sojka (1993).
[17] For interesting empirical proofs of this, see: Pinto et al. (1993) or Szanyi (1994).

With the exception of Hungary and Poland, the second basic element of the establishment of hard budget constraint, i.e. bankruptcy, was not really exercised in the observed countries. The Hungarian experience with bankruptcy is, however, rather promising. True, the introduction of bankruptcy procedures was a must in 1992, since the lack of payment discipline and the sudden increase of payment arrears reached a point of being dangerously disintegrational. Now, the same phenomenon is happening to practically all of the transforming economies.[18]

Techniques of liquidating the serious corporate (inter-company) indebtedness are numerous. Debt forgiveness, debtor and creditor consolidation, state-initiated restructuring programmes are the most important ones. Three debtor consolidation programmes failed in the Czech Republic (former Czechoslovakia) after 1990. The 1992 Hungarian consolidation programme failed completely and the results of the 1993–1994 second consolidation programme also failed in terms of successful corporate reorganization. Polish experiences of state assisted bank and debtor consolidation were somewhat more promising in 1994. Here more active and more effective methods of debt management were applied. Other countries are also preparing their consolidation programmes.

The basic reason for the failure of the previous consolidation programmes in all countries was that they were not seriously bound to the development and execution of the overwhelming restructuring plans. Restructuring should have been aimed at structural, technological, managerial modernization and at the change of the ownership structure. Briefly, restructuring should have contained all the necessary adjustment steps that companies failed to take prior to consolidation. There is, of course, little reason to expect companies to take the adjustment steps if they expect regular, active state intervention.

Reorganization plans were a necessary precondition of participating in both the 1993 Polish and Hungarian debtor and bank consolidation programmes. Thus, substantial changes in corporate structure and management are institutionally required from debtors. But the current poor performance of the 13 large Hungarian loss-makers, which were "reorganized" in the framework of the Ministerial Restructuring Project in 1992, indicates that central, not immanent, organic approaches are not very successful. There is little reason to think that commercial banks, which must reinforce companies to develop reorganization plans and which are also entitled to assess the companies' viability, could do this job more successfully than the state authorities. Nevertheless, banks do not have much practical industrial experience either.[19] Anyway, repeated consolidation programmes may further destroy payment discipline and threaten the positive results of Hungarian bankruptcy procedures as well for which this country paid a fairly high price.

Governments of the region seem to prefer active involvement in corporate restructuring. The argument is that it is the state that (also as owner) may be powerful enough to carry out and finance the huge tasks of restructuring. Bankruptcy is not applicable because of the serious losses it causes. Consolidation in itself cannot force companies (managers) to take adjustment steps. The state should also improve the quality of the companies before privatization. Such policies are carried out or are seriously considered

---

[18] The size of corporate indebtedness approaches in most countries a large part of the GDP. The only country where this measure showed rapid decline after 1992 was Hungary. The introduction of the bankruptcy procedures substantially limited the level of corporate arrears.

[19] True, both the Polish and the Hungarian bank consolidations enhanced the creation and development of workout departments in commercial banks. They may play a more active role in enforcing the restructuring of their biggest debtors.

in the majority of the transforming economies. Ministries for restructuring are established (e.g. in Romania), or the former branch ministries are charged with similar functions (e.g. in Russia).

We dare not say that extensive state involvement may reproduce the very same economic and decision-making structures that were common in the socialist economic system. But excessive state involvement in corporate decision-making surely does not help the development of market economic frames and the gathering of market economic experiences of managers. Excessive state involvement may provide a resort to the old paternalistic practices.

If we try to forecast the development of the corporate sphere of the transforming economies, we have to state first that for the companies, the most important factor for improvement is an increase in sales opportunities. Disorganization of the countries of the CIS (Commonwealth of Independent States) should be stopped and much better access to the markets of the developed economies should be provided. Unfortunately, neither of these two factors seem to be improving now.

With disadvantageous conditions continuing, two likely ways of corporate adjustment can be foreseen. The first one is a path to the gradual introduction of all the necessary elements of a market economy. The size of the state sector will be continuously reduced (through privatization and liquidation) and will be well defined. State asset management will be carried out in a market conform manner. Basic economic laws and regulations will apply equally for the state and the private sectors.

The second scenario is a backward one. The role of the state will be increased further and in the long run, the state sector will remain with a 60–80% employment level. The state sector will be exempted from some of the economic regulations. State bureaucrats' role in corporate decision-making will remain the same as under socialism. Due to the heavy losses produced by the inefficient state companies, development resources will remain scarce. Modernization, consumption and living standards will not be enhanced much.

In the case of the Czech Republic, Hungary, Poland and Slovenia, this second scenario is no longer an option. Despite the huge problems still ahead (e.g. in corporate restructuring), these economies had either reached the turning point or still have considerable reserves to cope with these problems (as in the Czech Republic). Slovakia and Croatia, and possibly the Baltic states are on the threshold. There are promising positive political changes in these countries, that may influence the development path of their economies toward the first scenario. The Balkan countries as well as the CIS countries seem to follow the second scenario now.

References

Alchian, A. – Demsetz, H. (1972): Production, Information Costs and Economic Organization. *A.E.R.* No. 62.
Dabrowski, J. – Federowicz, M. – Levitas, A. (1990): State Enterprise Adjustment. The Research Centre for Marketing and Property Reform in Gdansk. *Economic Transformation Papers,* No. 4.
Dabrowski, J. – Federowicz, M. – Szomburg, J. (1992): *Privatization of the Polish State-Owned Enterprises.* The Second Report, The Gdansk Institute for Market Economics.
Fama, E. F. (1980): Agency Problems and the Theory of the Firm. *Journal of Political Economics.* 88, No. 2 (April 1980).
Grosfeld, I. – Roland, G. (1995): Defensive and Strategic Restructuring in Central European Enterprises. CEPR Discussion Paper, No. 1135.

Hanke, S. (ed.) (1987): *Privatization and Development.* International Centre for Economic Growth, ICS Press.

Hunya, G. (1993): A Progress-Report on Privatization in Central and Eastern Europe. Paper presented at the XVth Session of the Workshop on European Economic Interaction and Integration, Vienna, 21 – 25 November, 1993.

Jensen, M.C. – Meckling, W.H. (1976): Theory of the Firm: Managerial Behaviour, Agency Costs and Ownership Structure. *Journal of Financial Economics,* No. 3/4.

Lipton, D. – Sachs, J. (1990): Privatization in Eastern Europe. The Case of Poland. *Brookings Papers on Economic Activity,* No. 2.

Mizsei, K. (1993): *Bankruptcy and the Post-Communist Economies of East-Central Europe.* Institute of East-West Studies.

Pinto, B. – Belka, M. – Krajewski, S. (1993): Transforming State Enterprises in Poland: Evidence on Adjustment by Manufacturing Firms. *Brookings Papers on Economic Activity,* No. 1.

Rapacki, R. (1991): Privatization in Transition Economies. Case Study of Poland. Working Paper, World Economy Research Institute, Warsaw School of Economics.

Rostowski, J. (1993): The Inter-Enterprise Debt Explosion in the Former Soviet Union: Causes, Consequences, Cures. London School of Economics, Centre for Economic Performance. Discussion Paper No. 142.

Sojka, M. (1993): Current State of Economic Transition in the Czech Republic and Possible Future Developments. Paper presented at ICEG RRT Core Group Meeting, Warsaw, October 21–23, 1993.

Szanyi, M. (1992): What Happened to the Transition in Hungary? An Approach from the Management Side. Institute for World Economics of the Hungarian Academy of Sciences, Working Paper No. 11.

Szanyi, M. (1993): The Liquidity Crisis and Bankruptcy Procedures in Hungary. Paper presented at the Institute for World-West Studies Conference on Bankruptcy, Warsaw, 11–14 April, 1993.

Szanyi, M. (1994): Adaptation by Hungarian Firms During the Transition Crisis. Institute for World Economics of the Hungarian Academy of Sciences, Working Paper No. 46.

Agriculture in East-Central Europe: crisis and transformation

JUDIT KISS

Agriculture has played a modest role in the economic and social transformation of the East-Central European countries, despite its internationally high significance in both generating GDP and providing employment.

The relatively insignificant role of the agrarian sector in the process of transformation can be explained by the fact that transformation has been concentrated on the regulatory and market system and on ownership relations rather than on structural and intra-sectoral changes. Furthermore, the process of transformation within the agrarian sector is blocked by the immanent crisis of the sector, which became apparent with the beginning of the transition. Actually, the transformation of agriculture can have more far-reaching social implications than that of the other economic sectors.

However, the development of efficient structures of agricultural production, marketing, processing and distribution is vital for the success of the entire economic and political transformation (Tracy 1993).

The crisis of agriculture

During the second half of the 1980s, the agricultural production of three East-Central European countries (Czechoslovakia, Hungary and Poland) showed significant fluctuations, resulting in declining growth rates at the time of transition. It became obvious that behind the statistical data based on distorted prices and exchange rates, a severe and deep agrarian crisis lay hidden. It was not only a production crisis characterized by falling output and caused by low and declining capital and labour efficiency, but it was also of a structural, institutional and ownership nature, not to mention the emerging sales problems.

The pre-transition agricultural crisis of the East-Central European countries has manifested itself in the following:

(a) A steady decrease of both the value and the volume of agricultural and food production and a severe decline of the livestock, leading to decreasing export commodity base and the emergence of scarcity in certain fields, and to increasing reliance on imports.

In 1992 grain production declined in Czechoslovakia, Hungary and Poland by 14%, 37% and 28%, respectively. Gross agricultural output declined by 10–17% in the East-Central European countries. In 1993 the fall continued, except in Poland where there was a slight increase. In 1994 Hungary and Slovakia showed some increase in agricultural output, while the Czech and the Polish production decreased (see Table 1).

Table 1
Real gross agricultural output
(1989 = 100)

	1990	1991	1992	1993	1994
Poland	94.5	93.0	82.9	84.5	78.6
Hungary	95.3	89.4	71.6	64.7	65.6
Czech Republic	97.7	89.0	78.3	76.4	72.2
Slovakia	92.8	85.9	74.0	68.4	74.6

Source: Agricultural Situation and Prospects in the Central and Eastern European Countries, European Commission, Brussels, 1995, p. 7.

The agricultural exports of the East-Central European countries have also decreased significantly after having reached a peak in 1991, which was caused by the decreasing domestic effective demand. At the same time, their agricultural imports increased and consequently the balance of their agricultural trade deteriorated. By 1993, both Poland and Slovakia ceased to exist as net agricultural exporters.

(b) The rapid opening of the so-called agricultural scissors, that is, a sharp shift in the domestic terms of trade due to the increment of farm input, fodder and energy prices and the lagging behind purchasing prices, resulted in low and deteriorating profitability and increasing losses of agricultural producers.

In both 1990 and 1991, the agricultural terms of trade deteriorated in Poland, Hungary and Slovakia, while in 1992 only the Polish and in 1993 only the Slovakian agricultural scissors opened further, while the Hungarian showed an improving tendency (Table 2).

Table 2
Changes of agricultural scissors in the East-Central European countries
(previous year = 100)

	1990	1991	1992	1993
Poland	132.4	141.0	108.0	97.0
Hungary	113.3	133.8	98.5	90.5
Slovakia	104.7	161.8	98.9	106.4

Source: *Népszabadság*, 18 March, 1994.

(c) The deteriorating efficiency of the utilization of productive forces, including land,[1] labour and capital, led to falling yields, low capacity utilization in the case of the food industries and the acceleration of the process of capital erosion and property exhaustion.

(d) The radical decrease of the self-financing capacity of agricultural production units led to decreased input use, the postponement of investments and maintenance, and the neglect of research and development.[2]

---

[1] In the case of Poland, the area of idle arable land increased from 1% of the arable land in 1989 to 9% in 1993.

[2] In Czechoslovakia, the share of agricultural investments within the total investments decreased from 12.6% in 1989 to 3.8% in 1992. In Poland, agricultural investment in 1991 fell by 50%. In Hungary, in the period 1991–1993 no significant agricultural investments were accomplished and even the ongoing investments were only maintained at a 70% level.

(e) The unprofitability, the increasing indebtedness, the losses and the bankruptcy of the majority of agricultural producers[3] resulted in increasing dismissals in the agricultural sector, hence in the emerging and growing agrarian and rural unemployment, and the impoverishment of the villages and the rural population.

*

The main causes of these crisis phenomena can be found in the economic development policy of the past; in the subordinated role of agriculture, leading to the exhaustion of agricultural, natural, human and capital resources; in the increasing and significant capital outflow from agriculture; and finally in the decrease of subsidies and other means of financial support.

The principle of efficiency has been neglected, since the main goals of agricultural production were: to reach (mainly food) self-sufficiency; to minimize or eliminate the imports of agricultural goods that could be produced domestically; and to generate export revenues from intra-regional trade. In addition, the rigidity of the agricultural enterprise structure – namely the predominance of large-scale state and collective farms in the case of Czechoslovakia and Hungary and the millions of small plots in the case of Poland – prevented the functioning of an efficiency criterion. An important part of agricultural output was produced with high costs and had to be heavily subsidized.

The immanent pre-transformation crisis of the agrarian sector became aggravated by the declining domestic demand for foodstuff.

The loss and/or narrowing of the traditional East-Central European markets and the uncertainties prevailing in alternative markets resulted in a sales crisis which weakened the financial position of agricultural enterprises and led to falling incomes in agriculture. This situation was even aggravated by the decreasing state subsidies.

However, the present agricultural development policy (or rather "no-policy") of the East-Central European countries is not so much directed at the elimination of the immanent crisis of the sector as it is aimed at placing agricultural production on a market basis and changing the ownership relations in favour of the private ownership of land and the means of production. The main question is whether these steps would lead to the recovery of agriculture or whether they would further deepen the agrarian crisis.

Market regulation

Among the main priorities of the transformation of agriculture in East-Central Europe, one can find the following: converting central planning to a market economy via liberalizing agricultural prices, lifting subsidies and financial support granted previously to the agricultural sector, liberalizing and de-monopolizing internal and foreign trade, putting agricultural production on a commercial basis in order to reduce the costs of agricultural output.

---

[3] In Poland 60% of the farms are on the verge of bankruptcy. In Hungary in 1992, 650 agricultural organizations (and one third of the agricultural co-operatives) went bankrupt and 100 of them were in the process of liquidation.

(a) In three countries of East-Central Europe (Poland, Hungary and Slovakia), the agricultural subsidies – compared to both the budget expenditures and the GDP – decreased by one half to two thirds during the period of 1990–1993 (Table 3).

Table 3
Agricultural subsidies in the East-Central European countries
(in per cent of budget expenditure and GDP)

	1990	1991	1992	1993	1994 estimate
In per cent of budget expenditure					
Poland	4.7	4.5	3.5	2.7	2.4
Hungary	9.1	3.7	3.3	3.6	3.7
Slovakia	18.4	8.2	7.8	6.4	5.7
In per cent of GDP					
Poland	1.3	1.3	0.9	0.8	0.8
Hungary	3.0	1.6	1.4	1.4	2.1
Slovakia	8.6	3.6	2.8	2.5	2.1

Source: *Népszabadság*, 18 March, 1994.

In the case of the Czech Republic, the level of agricultural subsidies (that is the so-called PSE – Producers' Subsidy Equivalent – indicator) declined from 40% in 1989 to 29% in 1990, to 13.5% in 1991 (Mertlik 1993) and to 10% in 1992 (Doucha 1994). Taking 1989 as 100, the amount of subsidies for agriculture from the state budget decreased to 32.4% in 1992, to 25.3% in 1993 and was expected to decrease to 18.7% in 1994 (Doucha 1994). The prices became liberalized in January 1993.

In Poland, the share of subsidies and other budget transfers to the food economy in total budget spendings decreased from 22.9% in 1989 to 8.7% in 1992 (Piskorz 1994). The prices were liberalized in January 1990.

The impact of price liberalization and the elimination of large subsidies for foodstuffs led to sharp price increases, which strongly diminished domestic demand, particularly for more expensive food products such as meat, milk and meat products. This resulted in an excess supply and sales crisis of some agricultural commodities and in further losses for agricultural enterprises. Furthermore, it should also be mentioned that rising food costs to consumers can increase the industrial production costs and can erode the competitiveness of the East-Central European countries (Tracy 1993).

Though in principle it was agreed by the East-Central European countries to introduce free agricultural prices, after a while it turned out that the outcome of this step was the further opening of the agricultural scissors, as the prices of inputs, e.g. energy, water and of processed products increased faster than the agricultural producers' prices, due to the still prevailing monopolistic position of input suppliers and the food processing industries.

Agricultural production costs have also increased due to the decreasing state subsidies and financial support caused by the increasing budget deficits of the East-Central European countries. These steps led not only to the decreasing profitability of their agricultural production, but also to their decreasing competitiveness on both internal and external markets.

(b) Consequently, a need has emerged in most of the East-Central European countries to introduce a market regulation system and to revise subsidy policy. The main tasks are to increase the security of production and marketing, to diminish the risks and uncertainties of producers and to increase the profitability of production via active state participation by

- providing fixed (guaranteed) prices for selected agricultural products,
- setting up production quotas,
- accomplishing the policy of intervention (through government purchases of the current excess, tactical exports–imports, public warehouses, indirect subsidies, etc.),
- providing more credits, and
- establishing agricultural market funds.

However, agrarian market regulation is only suitable for controlling production, but not for managing an agrarian crisis. Furthermore, the efficiency of the functioning of the market regulation system is greatly restricted by the poorly developed market infrastructure and the lack of proper market information (Piskorz 1994).

(c) In Hungary, the so-called agrarian market regulation system was introduced in April 1993. According to this system, the bread wheat, fodder maize, cow milk, pig and beef cattle markets are directly regulated by the system of guiding and guaranteed prices (plus a quota in the case of wheat), while the markets for poultry, sugar-beet and sunflower-seed are indirectly regulated via a monitoring system.[4]

The Hungarian Agricultural Market Regulation Regime[5] assigns an important role to the different Product Councils, that is, the organizations of agricultural producers, food producers, traders, different professional organizations and trade unions.

(d) In the Czech Republic, the State Fund for Market Regulation began functioning on January 1, 1993. Its main aim is to stabilize entrepreneurial conditions for primary agricultural producers via guaranteed prices. In fulfilling this role, the State Fund for Market Regulation uses declared minimum guaranteed prices, intervention purchases, subsidized exports and non-tariff protection of the domestic market against the import of agricultural products. Agricultural subsidies were expected to increase from 10% in 1992 to 12% in 1994 (Doucha 1994).

(e) In Poland, an Agricultural Market Agency was established in May 1990 for intervening in the agricultural market. Its activity focussed on:

- procurement and sales of agricultural and food products on domestic and foreign markets, in order to achieve price stabilization by using stock management policy, announcing interventionist prices or trade policy as the main instruments;
- management of strategic food reserves;
- providing the enterprises in difficulties with subsidies for export and with credit guarantees for the purchase of inventories.

Due to financial constraints, the Agency concentrates mainly on the grain market (in 1992 it bought some 52% of the total marketed crop) and to a smaller extent on the butter market. In early 1993, the Agency started to administer the market by distributing import quotas.

---

[4] On the Hungarian market regulation system see Halmai (1991, 1992).

[5] In 1993, HUF 35 billion were assigned for the operation of the agricultural market regime, HUF 26 billion were reserved for export subsidies and HUF 9 billion for intervention purposes. However, actually HUF 17 billion were spent on market intervention purposes.

Trade liberalization

The second pillar for establishing a market economy in the East-Central European countries is trade liberalization, that is, accomplishing a quasi-free trade in the case of agricultural products via lifting all the export and import restrictions, the non-tariff trade barriers, and reducing export subsidies and customs duties.

(a) However, as a consequence of decreasing profitability and actual production decline accompanied by the overvaluation of the national currencies, the East-Central European countries cannot make a real use of the liberalization of their export activities. Though the number of foreign trade companies multiplied, agricultural exports decreased, or at least stagnated, in spite of the fact that all the Visegrád countries have signed an Association Agreement with the EC (European Community), a free trade agreement with the EFTA (European Free Trade Association) and they have created a free trade area among themselves in the framework of the CEFTA (Central European Free Trade Agreement).[6]

It became obvious that the real results are more dependent on the competitiveness of exports and the agricultural subsidies than on free trade agreements. Consequently, there is a tendency in the East-Central European countries to revise their subsidy policies in accordance with those of the EC and the EFTA countries. All the more, as the agricultural products of the East-Central European countries should compete with EC, EFTA and USA products not only in the internal markets of these countries, but in the markets of the other East and Central European countries, including the states of the former Soviet Union as well.

(b) The other aspect of the opening up of the East-Central European agricultural markets is liberalizing the imports of agricultural goods via eliminating non-tariff import barriers and guaranteeing the free inflow of agricultural goods. The only import restrictions which remained were the customs, the licensing and the global quota system (in the case of Hungary and Poland), and chemical, sanitary and veterinary controls in the case of Czechoslovakia.

However, the experience of the first years of trade liberalization has shown that the markets of the East-Central European countries were left unprotected vis-à-vis the inflow of highly subsidized agricultural products of the developed countries and domestic producers were crowded out of the shrinking internal markets.

(c) In order to protect the domestic markets and the interest of domestic agricultural producers, many of the East-Central European countries decided to revise their trade liberalization policy in favour of more severe market protection via:
  • increasing customs duties, as happened in the case of Czechoslovakia and Poland;
  • introducing countervailing duties;
  • applying different levies, "special customs payments", supplementary import duties,[7] anti-dumping procedures and temporary suspension of import;
  • introducing a more strict system of import and export licences, import ban and/or new quantitative import quotas.

In most of the East-Central European countries, the new market protection measures are accompanied by strengthening their export promotion.

---

[6] On this issue see Tracy (1994).

[7] In the case of the former Czechoslovakia, since January 1, 1992 at the rate of 10%, and also in Poland since January 1, 1994.

Landownership, land use
and organizational structure

(a) The most significant issue of the transformation of the East-Central European agricultures is that of ownership relations. The main aim of this transformation is to change the ownership structure in favour of private ownership vis-à-vis the predominant state and collective (co-operative) ownership of land and the means of production.

There is general agreement that the rigid structure of landownership prior to transition should be eliminated, both the state farms and the co-operatives should be transformed and private ownership should be strengthened. However, it is not clear how to change the socialist forms of large-scale agricultural production units into effective privatized production units.

In East-Central Europe, almost 60% of the total agricultural land is to be involved. With the exception of Poland, the envisaged changes relate to a land area significantly larger than the amount of land involved in the post-1945 land reform of the countries concerned. For this reason alone, it is not difficult to predict that land-related issues will continue to shape the socio-economic life of the region for many years.

Though there is an agreement with regard to the principle of ownership transformation, there is a great variety as far as the forms of implementation are concerned. The differences are deriving, on the one hand, from the past ownership structures of the countries and, on the other hand, from the motives of the different political powers that play a part in the transformation.

(b) In Czechoslovakia in 1989, the 174 state farms and the 1024 agricultural co-operatives were exploiting 94.1% of the agricultural land (63.8% by the co-operatives and 30.3% by the state farms). The remaining 5.9% included private farms and school farms. Though 94% of land was used by co-operatives and state farms, land had formally remained in private hands even in communist times. As industrialization progressed over the decades, peasants left their land in the co-operatives when they moved into towns. Consequently, approximately 50% of the land used by the co-operatives were formally owned by city dwellers who were not members.

The Land Act of 1991 froze the given ownership situation in order to prevent selling any property prior to adopting the Co-operative Transformation Act. The law on co-operatives set the end of 1992 as the deadline for peasants to decide whether or not to leave the co-operatives; for the land and assets to be returned to the rightful owners; and for the transformation of the co-operatives.

In the Czech Republic, all co-operatives met these requirements, the large majority of the co-operatives were transformed into different entrepreneurial legal forms. The share of agricultural co-operatives in total Czech farmland decreased from almost 60% in 1991 to around 50% by 1994.

Privatization of state farms was scheduled to begin in 1993 in both the Czech and the Slovak Republic in the context of "large privatization". Their privatization was mainly hindered by their low efficiency, deep competitive disability and contemporary insolvency, resulting in uninterestedness in their shares from the side of the public and the Investment Privatization Funds. However, the privatization process speeded up and by early 1994 the share of state farms in total agricultural area decreased to 15%, while at the beginning of 1995 to below 5%.

The Land Law of May 1991 in the former Czechoslovakia envisaged the restitution of usufruct rights over land to former owners or their legal heirs, provided they were resident citizens and they had staked out their claim by the end of 1992. Simultaneously, several restitutional acts became effective and the process of "natural restitution", i.e. returning the physical property to its original owners started.

In spite of legislative and financial obstacles, in the period of 1991–1993 more than 58,000 individual farms were established in Czechoslovakia, comprising 23% of the total farmland area. Relatively large farms (over 100 hectares) are operating on 55% of the total acreage of individual farms (Vojteck 1994). The share of agricultural co-operatives in the farmland decreased from 59.8% in 1991 to 50.4% in 1993, the share of state farms decreased from 24.9% to 11.0% and the share of individual farms increased from 1.4% to 22.9% in the same period. The majority of private farms are operating with an average size of two hectares and are mainly producing for self-supply and not for the market.

However, the results of the transformation of the agricultural co-operatives are ambiguous. The initial de-collectivization effort of the government was not successful, at least from the formal (juridical) point of view. The large, concentrated agricultural co-operative continues to be a typical Czech agricultural enterprise. While in April 1993 the average acreage of a Czech agricultural co-operative after transformation was 4632, about 9000 private farmers work on an average of 112 acres (Mertlik 1993).

According to estimates, market oriented agriculture in the Czech Republic will be based on large agricultural enterprises (agricultural co-operatives or large individual farms based on hired labour) and not on family farms typical in the EU.

(c) In Hungary in May 1989, at the beginning of transformation, 31.7% of the arable land was owned by the state, 61.0% was in the use or possession of co-operatives and 7.3% was in the form of individual or auxiliary holdings (Harcsa 1991). During the first years of the systemic changes, no radical transformation occurred in the ownership and farm structure of the Hungarian agriculture. In 1991, 27% of the arable land was still owned by the state, 42% by co-operative members collectively, 27% by co-operative members individually and only 7% by private farmers.

The transformation of ownership in the agrarian sector was based on three pillars: namely, on the realization of the four Compensation Acts, on the transformation of the agricultural co-operatives and on the privatization of the state farms and food industry companies (Kiss 1993a, 1993b).

According to the Compensation Acts, the previous owners or their heirs have a right to obtain access to land via auctioning their compensation vouchers. About 500–700,000 persons are estimated to have claims for cropland; however, only 300–400,000 persons would like to obtain their compensation in kind. The land territory to be distributed among the owners of compensation vouchers is estimated to be around 1.5–2.0 million hectares. According to preliminary estimates, only 20% of the reclaimed land will be tilled by the new owners themselves, while the majority of lands will be offered for leasing to individuals or co-operatives. As a consequence, more than a million smallholders are expected to emerge on a territory of 5–6 million hectares (Varga 1993).

As far as the transformation of the 1386 Hungarian agricultural co-operatives are concerned, by the end of 1992, 1207 co-operatives, with a total territory of 5.6 million hectares, had been transformed formally into a holding company, a public or private limited company based on private ownership of land and the joint activity of the members. One hundred and seventy-nine co-operatives failed to be transformed due to time constraints or bankruptcy.

Following the process of property designation, around 90% of the members of the co-operatives have opted for remaining within the framework of the transformed co-operatives. Individual and/or group secession and splitting and cessation have affected only 15–20% of the co-operatives' combined property. Around 25–40,000 persons have withdrawn from the co-operatives and 6–10% of the previous members have opted to become private farmers on a total of 105,000 hectares of privately owned land, with 5–10 hectares each, which was withdrawn from the co-operatives.

Out of the 124 Hungarian agricultural state farms with a total arable land of 902,000 hectares, 25 state farms with a territory of 154,000 hectares are envisaged to remain in majority state ownership, while 83 state farms with a territory of 550,000 hectares will remain under the umbrella of the State Property Agency and the State Property Management Co. These state farms will be transformed into business societies and joint stock companies in the course of privatization. A property with a value of HUF 35 billion has been designated for privatization out of the total property of HUF 100 billion belonging to the state farms.

The low speed of the privatization of state farms is due to the lack of market for croplands, the low technological level and the high indebtedness of the state farms, let alone the decreasing demand for agricultural products.

(d) In Poland, the main issue is not the privatization of agricultural lands, as Polish agriculture is characterized by the high share (80%) of private ownership of land. There are more than 3 million small peasant plots with an average size of 6.4 hectares. In 1990, 29.6% of the private farms were below an average size of 2 hectares and only 17.6% were above the average size of 10 hectares (Orbánné 1992). Most of the small farms are based on part-time farming and produce with low efficiency.

According to optimistic estimates (Herer – Sadowski 1993), by the year 2000 the number of private farms will be reduced by one third, shifting about one fifth of the arable lands from farms with less than 10 hectares to those whose area exceeds 20 hectares. Consequently, the average farm size would exceed 8 hectares.

Collective ownership in Polish agriculture was practically limited to 2000–2500 state farms, comprising 19–20% of the arable land and employing a total of some 400,000 people. Their privatization and commercialization are greatly hindered by their poor financial situation (producing loss, insolvency and high indebtedness), low profitability deriving from high costs of production and low efficiency, unfavourable location (they are heavily concentrated in Western Poland) and lack of local capital.

In 1991, some 40 state farms were scheduled for liquidation on account of their economic performance and 77 were declared bankrupt. By 1994 a total of 253 agricultural enterprises were liquidated and their land sold, leased or transferred rent-free.

In January 1992, legislation came into force, according to which the privatization of all state-owned real estates was to be concluded within the next two years. All agricultural real estates were taken over by a Treasury-controlled Agricultural Property Fund and were disposed of in various ways to private, institutional or individual investors.

In 1993 the Treasury Agricultural Property Agency took over 1.88 million hectares of land belonging to state farms. Of this acreage only 58,600 hectares were sold. The state farms taken over by the Agency were turned into treasury-owned farming enterprises. The Agency also took possession of buildings containing 276,000 dwelling units. Of these 42,000 have been sold.

The role of the 2000 co-operatives was negligible, as they occupied only 4% of the arable land.

(e) One of the common features of settling the land issue in the East-Central European countries is to provide a kind of justice and compensation to the former landowners for moral and ethical reasons via restituting property that was earlier confiscated or via compensation (that is, providing compensation vouchers to the previous owners or to their heirs, which they could use, among other purposes, for buying land). The main danger here is that the resulting fragmentation of agricultural production might have adverse effects on the efficiency and competitiveness of the agrarian sector, let alone the fact that compensation could put pressure on current or future government budgets.

The other common feature is the de-collectivization of agriculture, that is, the endeavour to transform the large and centrally regulated agricultural co-operatives into smaller and more efficient units, different types of business organizations, limited liability and joint stock companies operating on market principles. The main issues are: what will the nature of the transformed agricultural co-operatives be like? Will they be in the future "true" co-operatives, corresponding to the Western notion of a co-op or will they rather behave like public or private companies?

However, the main task ahead of the East-Central European agricultural transformation is the privatization of state farms, which had a significant role in both agricultural production and landownership. The process of privatization of state farms is hindered mainly by the lack of capital, the low profitability of agricultural production and the present uncertainties of the landownership system due to the lack of a proper land law in some of the countries (e.g. Hungary).

The process of transforming the landownership system is highly complicated. In the absence of proper cadasters and established land prices, land assessment is indispensable. There is a great deal of uncertainty regarding the heavily indebted co-operatives, state farms and food processing companies. Where restitution is the main element of the land reform, numerous problems have emerged from the fact that applications are based on affidavits instead of missing title deeds. Given the slow progress in decision-making, millions of farmers are now cultivating their lands without proper title deeds, while tens of thousands of co-operatives and state farms continue to operate in a "no future" environment.

Most of the new landowners are eager to rent their new property and collect a land rent, or convert it into capital asset in some agricultural enterprise. However, in the case of peasants, there is more willingness to cultivate the land on a contract basis as opposed to owning it, because ownership is often linked to cultivation obligation. Consequently, there is a tendency for a diversion of landownership from land use. Moreover, the marketability of land is generally limited. Foreigners cannot buy it at all and even domestic investors are prevented from creating large estates.

It is thus likely that the transformation process will adversely affect agricultural production in the short run.

(f) After having accomplished the restitutions, the compensations, the transformation of the co-operatives and the privatization of the state farms, the main issues will be as follows: what kind of agricultural units will emerge within the East-Central European countries, what organizational forms will dominate the agriculture of the region and will they be more competitive than those that existed previously.

Though only few years have passed since the beginning of the transformation of East-Central European agriculture, there are certain tendencies to be foreseen:

• the share of private ownership of land will increase, though not at the same rate and speed as envisaged by the governments initiating the transformation;

• landownership will be separated from land use due to the politically motivated restitution and compensation acts, consequently, a new land tenure system will emerge in East-Central Europe;[8]

• a process of land concentration will start, whereby fragmented land holdings will merge into larger, more viable units;

• a mixture of differing landownership and land use forms – that is, differing organizational forms and firm structures – will emerge within the East-Central European agricultures, covering the millions of small plots of 1–2 hectares based on family labour, the thousands of family farms of some tens of hectares, the transformed and de-collectivized agricultural co-operatives of 300–500 hectares, the privately owned farm-estates of some hundreds of hectares and the state-owned, large-scale big farms, as well as different forms of land lease (Kiss 1993b).

Financing agricultural transformation

As one of the main causes of the present East-Central European agricultural crisis is the outflow of capital from agriculture, resulting in property exhaustion and the lack of investments, the development of agriculture and the emergence of viable farms and firms are indispensable for decreasing and eliminating the lack of capital[9] and solving the problem of financing the agrarian sector.

Presently the financing of agriculture is restricted by the following factors:

• the lack and/or insufficient functioning of a decentralized rural banking system;

• the lack of proper banking guarantees, due to the uncertainties of the landownership and land tenure system;

• the low profitability and the deteriorating liquidity of the agricultural producers.

As agricultural production is considered an unattractive and risky business with low profitability, most of the commercial banks are unwilling to supply credits or only at high interest rates against strict guarantee requirements.

In order to solve the problem of agricultural financing, the following requirements should be met:

• the establishment of the necessary financial infrastructure in the rural areas;

• the quick and reassuring settlement of the landownership relations;

• the active participation of the state via the introduction of mortgage, public warehouses, state credit guarantee and by way of providing interest rate preferences;

• the increment of the profitability of agricultural production and the establishment of viable and efficient production units in order to provide financial security in the case of credit granting and to decrease the risks and costs of credit supply.

---

[8] In the case of Hungary, 80–90% of the new landowners do not intend or are not able to cultivate their land, as they are old or pensioners or urban dwellers.

[9] The present fixed capital need of Hungarian agriculture is estimated to be around HUF 360 billion, while the medium term investment requirement is around HUF 200–250 billion.

However, the experience of the highly developed countries shows that the problem of agricultural financing cannot be solved by market forces alone. It requires active state participation and budget support, depending on the role designated to the agrarian sector.

The social impact of agricultural transformation

(a) Taking into account the relatively large share of agriculture in total employment, the relatively low labour productivity and the objective to increase efficiency, there is a tendency of increasing outflow of labour from the agricultural sector.

In the case of the former Czechoslovakia, the number of workers employed by agricultural co-operatives decreased by 40% (from 308,000 to 182,000) between 1991 and 1993, and the number of workers employed by the state farms by almost 50% (from 95,000 to almost 48,000).

In Poland, agricultural employment decreased only slightly (from 4.425 to 4.037 million) between 1990 and 1992, because no significant structural changes occurred (Gorzelak – Jalowiecki 1993). However, according to some estimates (Herer – Sadowski 1993), the workforce employed in Polish private farms will decrease by 440,000 persons till the year 2000.

In Hungary, while 840,000 people were employed by the agricultural sector in 1980, their number decreased to 550,000 by 1990 and to 423,000 by 1991. Between 1992 and 1994 agricultural employment decreased by a further 38%. In 1993 the number of rural unemployed was around 100,000.

(b) In order to avoid the sudden and significant increase in agricultural unemployment – especially in the case of Poland –, priority should be given to labour-intensive techniques in agricultural production. Rural development should include the deployment of supporting industries and services.

(c) A further social problem is the increasing differentiation and polarization of the rural areas due to the change of ownership relations and the functioning of the market forces. One can see the appearance of a well-to-do stratum of agricultural entrepreneurs and/or landlords on the one side, while on the other the emergence of landless, agricultural workers. Between the two poles one could find small, private producers cultivating their own piece of land; small farmers cultivating family-owned or leased land; middle farmers cultivating some 10 hectares of land and employing hired labour; owners of some 100 hectares of land estates; and the employees of state-owned or privately owned big estates, and of agricultural enterprises.

Prospects and the tasks ahead

It is obvious that the significance and the share of the agricultural sector in the national economy of the East-Central European countries will decrease within both the GDP and total employment, due to the possibility of a more dynamic development of the other sectors and the probability of contraction of primary agricultural production.

According to estimates, the Czech agricultural employment will decrease by 7.2% yearly between 1993 and 2000, and by 3.0% yearly between 2000 and 2005, while agricultural output will decrease by 1.4% and increase by 0.9%, respectively (Sojka et al. 1993).

In the case of Poland, the share of agriculture and forestry within the GDP will decrease from 6.8% in 1993 to 4.5% by the year 2005, due to the relatively slow increase in domestic demand for food and that of export markets for Polish agricultural goods. The share of agriculture in total employment will fall from 33.8% in 1992 to 18.2% by 2005 (Gorzelak – Jalowiecki 1993).

In the case of Hungary, the share of agricultural employment in the total is expected to decrease from 13.9% in 1992 to 10–11% by the year 2005, while the contribution of agriculture to the GDP is expected to decrease from 15% in 1989 and 9% in 1992 to 7% by the year 2005 (Ehrlich – Révész 1995).

It is quite probable that the agricultural crisis will continue through the middle of the 1990s, reaching a point of stabilization around 1996–1997, and a modest development might start in the second half of the 1990s. The first period will be characterized by a deep and rapid slump of agricultural output, employment and area of the exploited agricultural land, whereas minor restructuring is expected to occur mainly in the second period.

It will be very difficult to preserve a net exporter position for many of the East-Central European countries, while the Czech Republic is expected to become a net importer of agricultural and food products.

As far as the ownership and farm structures of the East-Central European agricultures are concerned, the present results of the transformation make it probable that agricultural co-operatives will maintain a significant portion of agricultural land both in the case of the Czech and the Slovak Republics and Hungary. The most promising future form of agricultural business is a combination of large-scale enterprises with the advantages of co-operatives and joint stock companies. Owing to the great need for capital in the agribusiness, private farms will probably merge into large companies or their mutual links may be strengthened through co-operative schemes, associations or holding-type enterprises.

Family farms will also develop, but the proportion of land farmed on this basis will hardly exceed 10–15% of the total farmland in the case of the Czech Republic and Hungary, because modern farming is capital-intensive and agricultural capital brings low returns. However, the share of private farms will remain significant in the case of Poland, as a consequence of the concentration of the present small plots into bigger units and the privatization of the state farms, though a considerable part of Polish farmers will continue to earn their livelihood by running small farms.

The main tasks ahead of the East-Central European countries are as follows:
• to adopt and accomplish a well-defined, transparent, detailed and targeted agricultural policy;
• to complete the transformation of and to settle ownership relations, including landownership, land use, land tenure and farm structures;
• to create a regulated market with government-adjusted time-lags between price changes and demand changes and related indirect subsidies;
• to restructure production;
• to increase the productivity and competitiveness of production.

References

Csáki, Cs. (1992): Transformation of Agriculture in Central and Eastern Europe and the Former USSR, Major Policy Issues and Perspectives, April 1992, The World Bank. Policy Research Working Papers.

Doucha, T. (1994): Czech Agricultural Policy and Agrarian Market and Their Impact on the Agricultural Sector after 1989. Manuscript, Research Institute of Agricultural Economics, Prague.

Ehrlich, É. – Révész, G. (1995): *Hungary and its Prospects, 1985–2005.* Akadémiai Kiadó, Budapest.

Gorzelak, G. – Jalowiecki, B. (1993): *Development of Poland Until the Year 2005.* Warszawa.

Halmai, P. (1991): Az agrárpiaci rendtartás kiépítésének lehetőségei (The possibilities of establishing a market regulation system). *Kereskedelmi Szemle,* 32/12.

Halmai, P. (1992): Agrárpiaci intézmények, terméktanácsok (Market regulation institutions, product councils). *Gazdálkodás,* XXXVI/12.

Harcsa, I. (1991): Privatization and Reprivatization in Hungarian Agriculture. *Acta Oeconomica,* vol. 43.

Herer, W. – Sadowski, W. (1993): Changes in Agrarian Structure in the Framework of Changes of the Structure and Size of Total Employment in the Economy. Manuscript.

Illner, M. – Machonin, P. – Müller, K. – Sojka, M. (1993): Czech Republic – Transformations After 1989 and Beyond. Scenario of Change until the Year 2005. Manuscript, Prague.

Kiss, J. (1993a): An Optimistic Scenario for the Hungarian Agriculture. Manuscript, Budapest.

Kiss, J. (1993b): Transformation and Privatization in the Hungarian Agriculture. Manuscript, Budapest.

Mertlik, P. (1993): Political Economy of Czech Agriculture. Prague, Institute of Sociology.

Orbánné Nagy M. (1992): *A volt KGST-térség országainak agrárkereskedelmi helyzete és a jövőbeni együttműködés lehetőségei. Lengyelország* (The state of agricultural trade of the former CMEA countries and the prospects for future co-operation. Poland). Agrárgazdasági Kutató és Informatikai Intézet, Budapest.

Piskorz, W. (1994): Market Regulation, Price Support and Protectionism in Poland's Agriculture and Food Economy. Manuscript.

Sojka, M. – Kouba, K. – Nachtigal, V. – Hutar, J. (1993): Economic Scenario. The Czech Republic in 2005. Manuscript. Prague, Institute of Sociology.

Stanek, P. – Vaclavu, V. – Vaclavu, K. – Eremiás, V. (1993): Scenario of the Development of Agriculture in the Czech Republic. Manuscript. Prague, Institute of Sociology.

Swinnen, J. (1993): The Development of Agricultural Policies in Central and Eastern Europe: An Endogenous Policy Theory Perspective. Leuven Institute for Central and East European Studies, Katholieke Universiteit Leuven, *Food Policy,* No. 3.

Tracy, M. (1993): *Food and Agriculture in a Market Economy, An Introduction to Theory, Practice and Policy.* Agricultural Policy Studies, Brussels.

Tracy, M. (ed.) (1994): East–West European Agricultural Trade: The Impact of Association Agreements. Agricultural Policy Studies, Brussels.

Varga, Gy. (1993): A mezőgazdaság és a szövetkezetek átalakulása (The transformation of agriculture and the co-operatives). *Társadalmi Szemle,* No. 4.

Vojteck, V. (1994): EC Membership by the Year 2000: A Realistic Objective. Manuscript. Research Institute of Agricultural Economics, Czech Republic.